What the **Science of Reading Says**

Literacy Strategies
for Grades 1-2

Erica Bowers, Ed.D.

Shell Education

Contributing Author

Brenda Van Dixhorn, M.A.Ed.

Consultants

Jennifer Jump, M.A.
Jodene Lynn Smith, M.A.

Publishing Credits

Corinne Burton, M.A.Ed., *President* and *Publisher*
Aubrie Nielsen, M.S.Ed., *EVP of Content Development*
Véronique Bos, *Vice President of Creative*
Kyra Ostendorf, M.Ed., *Publisher, professional resources*
Cathy Hernandez, *Senior Content Manager*
Fabiola Sepulveda, *Junior Art Director*
Michelle Lee Lagerroos, *Interior Graphic Designer*
David Slayton, *Assistant Editor*

Image Credits

pp. 56, 88, 99, 102, 106 Miriam Lagerroos. All other images from iStock and/or Shutterstock.

Shell Education

A division of Teacher Created Materials

5482 Argosy Avenue
Huntington Beach, CA 92649

www.tcmpub.com/shell-education

ISBN 978-1-0876-9673-7

© 2024 Shell Educational Publishing, Inc.

Table of Contents

INTRODUCTION

What the Science of Reading Says

This book is one in a series of professional resources that provide teaching strategies aligned with the Science of Reading. The term *the Science of Reading* pervades the national conversation around the best literacy instruction for all students. The purpose of this series is to close the gap between the knowledge and understanding of what students need to become literate humans and the instructional practices in our schools. This gap is widely acknowledged yet remains intact. While research is available, journals are not easy to navigate. However, with concise resources that build understanding of the body of research and offer strategies aligned with that research, teachers can be equipped with the logical steps to find success. This book will help you navigate the important Science of Reading research and implement strategies based on that research in your classroom.

> The Science of Reading is the collection of excellent research that leads to the understanding of how students learn to read.

What is meant by the phrase *Science of Reading*? The Science of Reading is the collection of research that leads to the understanding of how students learn to read. Research dedicated to understanding how we learn to read and write has been conducted for more than fifty years. This research has explored topics ranging from the skills needed to read and write, to the parts of the brain involved in reading development, to the best way to teach children how to read. The research clearly demonstrates the following: 1) the most effective early reading instruction includes an explicit, structured, phonics-based approach to word reading; and 2) reading comprehension relies on word reading (being able to decode individual words) and language comprehension (being able to understand what words and sentences mean).

According to the Report of the National Reading Panel (2000), a comprehensive program of literacy instruction should contain explicit skills instruction in phonemic awareness, phonics, fluency, vocabulary, and reading and language comprehension. Effective literacy instruction includes explicit instruction in all five of the components of reading plus writing. Ideally, this will occur in classrooms that emphasize and facilitate motivation for and engagement in reading through the use of a variety of authentic texts, authentic tasks, cooperative learning, and whole- and small-group instruction that connects reading to students' lived realities. Motivation and engagement are important considerations in our teaching. Cultural and linguistic relevance and responsiveness are essential. Authentic opportunities for speaking, listening, and writing are critical. Gradual release of responsibility is necessary to build independence and is an integral part of promoting a culture of literacy that students will embrace and take with them once they leave our care. Let us explore more closely what we can learn from the Science of Reading.

The Science of Reading: Models of Reading

The widely accepted model of the Simple View of Reading (SVR) proposed by Gough and Tunmer (1986) and later refined by Hoover and Gough (1990) depicts reading comprehension as the product of word recognition and language comprehension. This model of reading offers educators a simple, comprehensible way of organizing their understanding of the constructs that can predict successful literacy outcomes (Snow 2018). Hoover and Tunmer (2018) describe these constructs this way:

- Word recognition: the ability to recognize printed words accurately and quickly to efficiently gain access to the appropriate word meanings contained in the internal mental lexicon.

- Language comprehension: the ability to extract and construct literal and inferred meaning from speech.

- Reading comprehension: the ability to extract and construct literal and inferred meaning from linguistic discourse represented in print.

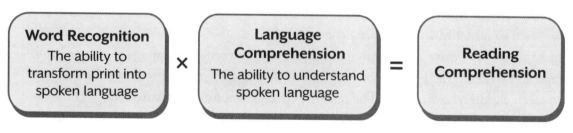

The Simple View of Reading

Later work (Hoover and Tunmer 2020; Scarborough 2001) further describes the crucial elements within each of these constructs by incorporating the best of what science tells us about how we read. Scarborough's Reading Rope identifies the underlying skills required for effective and efficient word recognition and language comprehension.

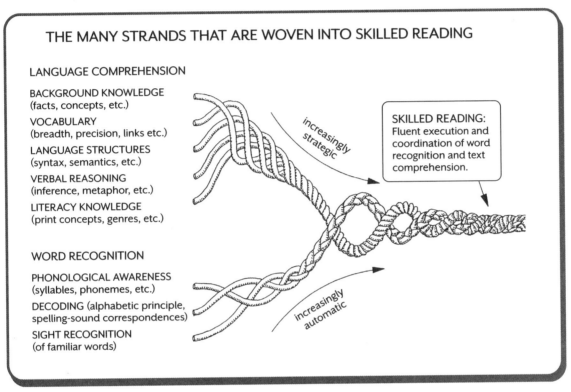

THE MANY STRANDS THAT ARE WOVEN INTO SKILLED READING

LANGUAGE COMPREHENSION

BACKGROUND KNOWLEDGE
(facts, concepts, etc.)
VOCABULARY
(breadth, precision, links etc.)
LANGUAGE STRUCTURES
(syntax, semantics, etc.)
VERBAL REASONING
(inference, metaphor, etc.)
LITERACY KNOWLEDGE
(print concepts, genres, etc.)

WORD RECOGNITION

PHONOLOGICAL AWARENESS
(syllables, phonemes, etc.)
DECODING (alphabetic principle, spelling-sound correspondences)
SIGHT RECOGNITION
(of familiar words)

increasingly strategic

increasingly automatic

SKILLED READING:
Fluent execution and coordination of word recognition and text comprehension.

Scarborough's Reading Rope

Credit: Hollis Scarborough, "Connecting Early Language and Literacy to Later Reading (Dis)abilities: Evidence, Theory, and Practice" in *Handbook of Research in Early Literacy*, edited by Susan B. Neuman and David K. Dickinson © Guilford Press, 2001.

Wesley Hoover, William Tunmer, Philip Gough, and Hollis Scarborough are psychologists who dedicated their research to understanding what reading is and what must be present or learned for reading to occur. They have described the SVR as *simple* because it is intended to focus our attention only on what is important in reading, not to explain the process of *how* reading happens. Similarly, Scarborough expanded on the SVR to focus attention on more specific details of language comprehension and word recognition such as prior knowledge and phonological awareness, attempting to include space for process with the addition of automaticity and strategy. Both the SVR and the Reading Rope are models—hypotheses that attempt to explain the phenomena of reading. The models describe necessary but not sufficient conditions for reading. Many teachers know that decoding skills can be present, language comprehension can be apparent, and yet comprehension can be impeded. These foundational models do not account for motivation, development, social-emotional considerations, linguistic differences, and a host of other factors relevant to literacy teaching and learning.

In the use and understanding of these models, one can see how the Science of Reading brings together expertise across disciplines. These models of skilled reading provide a roadmap for researchers and classroom educators for the development of instructional practices that promote these essential skills.

The Science of Reading: Implications for Teaching

Here is where we are wise to remember that the Science of Reading relies on the *sciences* of reading. It encompasses many fields. The modeling work of cognitive and educational psychologists informs the work of others in literacy research. The work of the literacy researchers informs the work of those who translate it into instructional practices. The end goal is to explain the processes by which successful reading occurs and the most effective ways to develop skills that enable these processes. As Louisa Moats declared, "Teaching reading is rocket science!" In this seminal piece, Moats describes how teachers can think about the Simple View of Reading in relation to their classroom practice:

> The implications of the Simple View of Reading should be self-evident: reading and language arts instruction must include deliberate, systematic, and explicit teaching of word recognition and must develop students' subject-matter knowledge, vocabulary, sentence comprehension, and familiarity with the language in written texts. Each of these larger skill domains depends on the integrity of its subskills. (Moats 2020, para. 11)

Moats's description reflects the recommendations of the National Reading Panel (NRP) (2000) and the modeling by the cognitive scientists. The evidence base from the sciences that inform our understanding of reading consistently supports systematic and direct instruction in the five components of reading: phonemic awareness, phonics, fluency, vocabulary, and comprehension.

Phonological Awareness and Phonemic Awareness

Phonological awareness is an umbrella term that refers to noticing and manipulating sounds in speech, for instance, individual words, syllables, and sounds in words. *Phonemic awareness*, a subcategory of phonological awareness, is the understanding that spoken words are made of individual sounds called *phonemes*. Research demonstrates that phonemic awareness can be taught and that this teaching is effective for a variety of learners (NRP 2000; National Early Literacy Panel 2008). It assists children in learning to read and learning to spell. Explicitly teaching children to manipulate phonemes, focused on one or two types of phoneme manipulations rather than multiple types, and teaching children in small groups are most effective (NRP 2000). According to the recommendations of the NRP report, children should receive approximately 18 hours of phonemic awareness instruction to learn these skills. This means teaching phonemic awareness every day; 18 hours over the course of a school year is about 6 minutes per day. Phonemic awareness instruction should occur in grades 1 and 2 as needed.

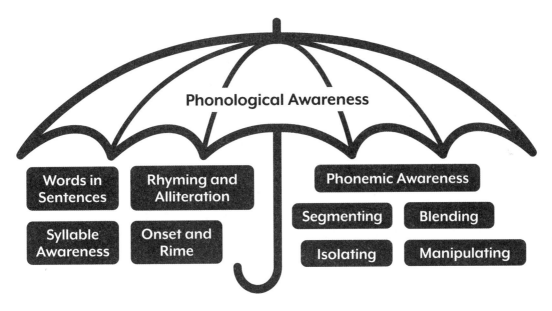

Phonics

Phonics is the term used to describe the relationships between the letters (graphemes) of written language and the individual sounds (phonemes) of spoken language. Phonics instruction helps children learn and use the alphabetic principle—the understanding that there are systematic and predictable relationships between written letters and spoken sounds (Armbruster, Lehr, and Osborn 2010). Children need knowledge of phonics to become efficient, automatic decoders of written text. Explicit, systematic instruction in phonics has been shown to be most effective, regardless of the approach used (NRP 2000). There are three approaches to teaching phonics: (1) *synthetic phonics*, which emphasizes teaching students to convert letters into sounds and then to blend sounds to form words; (2) *analytic phonics*, during which children do not pronounce sounds in isolation but rather learn to analyze letter-sound relationships in previously learned words; (3) a*nalogy-based phonics*, in which children learn to use parts of word families they know to recognize unknown words which may contain the same parts. Explicit and systematic instruction in phonics provides students instruction in letter-sound (grapheme-phoneme) connections. This graphophonemic knowledge is essential for mastery of decoding. Students must be provided instruction that engages the opportunity to hear, say, read, and spell words both in and out of context. This instruction should happen daily, for at least 30 to 45 minutes for students in grades K through 2. While not all children need intensive phonics instruction, no student is harmed by or will have their reading progress impeded by receiving phonics instruction. Many students will benefit significantly from systematic phonics instruction in grades K through 2.

> Children need knowledge of phonics to become efficient, automatic decoders of written text. Explicit, systematic instruction in phonics has been shown to be most effective.

Fluency

Fluency is defined as the ability to read with speed, accuracy, and proper expression. It is a critical component of skilled reading. Fluency depends upon well-developed word recognition skills that readers can apply to silent reading or reading aloud that make word reading rapid, accurate, and cognitively efficient. When children are fluent readers, they spend less time trying to decode or pronounce words and better attend to the comprehension of text. However, fluency also represents a level of expertise beyond word recognition (NRP 2000). Phrasing, intonation, and monitoring reading are all considered fluency skills. Research demonstrates that students benefit from fluency instruction and that reading comprehension may be aided by fluency (NRP 2000).

Vocabulary

Vocabulary refers to the words we must understand to communicate effectively. Vocabulary plays an important role in reading comprehension. Children who develop strong vocabularies and continue to deepen and broaden their vocabulary knowledge find it easier to comprehend more of what they read, especially as text becomes more complex (Sinatra, Zygouris-Coe, and Dasinger 2012). Moreover, students who have strong vocabularies have less difficulty learning unfamiliar words because those words are likely to be related to words that students already know (Rupley, Logan, and Nichols 1999). Researchers and educators often refer to and consider four types of vocabulary: *listening vocabulary* consists of the words we need to know to understand what we hear; *speaking vocabulary* consists of words we use to speak; *reading vocabulary* refers to the words we need to understand what we read; and *writing vocabulary* is the words we use in writing (Armbruster, Lehr, and Osborn 2010).

> Children who develop strong vocabularies and continue to deepen and broaden their vocabulary knowledge find it easier to comprehend more of what they read.

Research reveals that most vocabulary is learned indirectly, but some must be taught directly (Armbruster, Lehr, and Osborn 2010). Vocabulary instruction should be direct and explicit.

Comprehension

Research repeatedly demonstrates that students benefit greatly from both direct, explicit instruction in reading comprehension strategies and instruction in other areas that support reading comprehension (Duke, Ward, and Pearson 2021; Duke and Pearson 2002; Durkin 1978; Pressley and Afflerbach 1995). The NRP (2000) identified a number of effective strategies for teaching comprehension. These strategies include vocabulary development, prediction skills (including inferencing), the building of a broad base of topical knowledge, the activation of prior knowledge, think-alouds, visual representations, summarization, and questioning. Students also need to develop their metacognitive skills to become strategic and independent readers. Metacognitive skills, also referred to as *metacognition*, are most simply understood as thinking about one's thinking. This includes skills such as self-questioning, making connections, predicting, and visualizing. Most literacy researchers agree that metacognition plays a significant role in reading comprehension (Baker and Brown 1984; Gourgey 1998; Hacker, Dunlosky, and Graesser 1998; Palincsar, Sullivan, and Brown 1987). Research shows that teachers should foster metacognition and comprehension monitoring during comprehension instruction, because in doing so, students will learn to monitor and self-regulate their ability to read.

Throughout this book, we delve more deeply into each of these areas to share and explain the research as it applies to specific areas of reading development and to students of different grade levels.

Components of Literacy

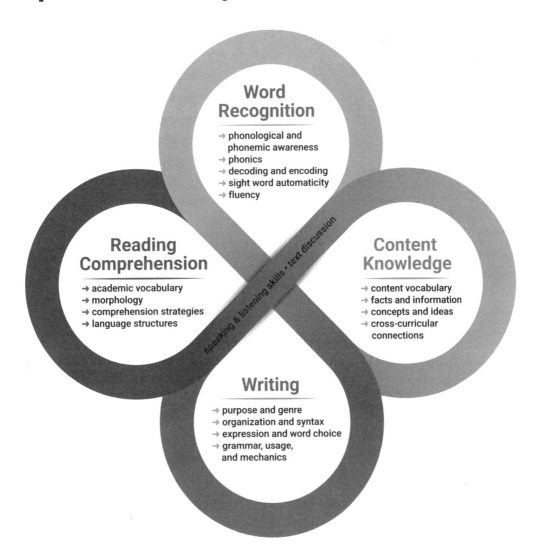

The figure on page 7 reflects what we know to be the essential components of comprehensive literacy instruction. This visual representation of the Science of Reading brings together what we know from multiple sciences of reading and literacy, from research in early literacy, from research on the reading-writing connection, from the national reports on reading and literacy, and from the cognitive sciences. Development of skills in word recognition, comprehension, content knowledge, and writing are well supported in the research as effective practices for literacy instruction. The figure includes the five components of reading recommended by the NRP, however the reorganization of these components into the four constructs is intentional, representing the evolution in our understanding of the connections between reading and the wider consideration of what it means to be literate. Just as the SVR was intended to call our attention to the components of reading comprehension (Hoover and Tunmer 2022), the subcategories describing each component of this model give us guidance as to where to focus our teaching in order to support skilled reading and literacy development.

The inclusion of *content knowledge* as a separate construct is important in this model. Research has long struggled over the role of content knowledge in reading comprehension. We are well aware of the fact that the activation and development of prior knowledge (schema) is important to comprehension; we know that knowledge of words and word parts plays a key role in the decoding of new and/or unfamiliar words and determining the meaning of such words. Of primary importance for activating prior knowledge is the presence of relevant knowledge. There is a growing body of research that demonstrates the critical role of content knowledge in comprehension of text concerning that topic. In fact, the knowledge a reader brings (content and word knowledge) is the primary determinant of comprehension (Anderson and Pearson 1984; Cabell and Hwang 2020). Content knowledge can support readers in making inferences and connections to text. This can deepen understanding of a text and support learning as readers are better able to connect what they read in text to existing schema in ways that develop new learning (Cabell and Hwang 2020). Cabell and Hwang's (2020) recent review of research on content-rich literacy instruction demonstrates its important role in developing language and knowledge in support of reading comprehension. The inclusion of content knowledge as a separate and co-important construct in this model also serves as an important reminder that the Science of Reading goes beyond the narrow discussion of skills-based decoding instruction and that our literacy instruction should be embedded in meaningful context.

> There is a growing body of research that demonstrates the critical role of content knowledge in comprehension of text concerning that topic.

Including **writing** as a component in the model draws attention to the important role writing plays in literacy development and the reciprocal relationship writing shares with reading. Decades of research demonstrate that direct and explicit teaching of writing skills, strategies, and processes is effective at improving students' writing and communication skills (Graham et al. 2012b). There is great benefit to bringing reading and writing study and practice together (Graham 2020). Reading and writing draw from a shared set of literacy knowledge and skills, including vocabulary development, background knowledge, and an understanding of syntax, semantics, and morphology. Additionally, reading across genres to understand how one communicates in a particular genre can inform writing in that genre. Writing in response to reading makes comprehension "visible" as students summarize, explain, infer, and make connections to what they have read.

Finally, wrapping the components of this literacy model in a "ribbon" of speaking and listening serves as a powerful reminder that speaking and listening are essential to literacy development. Though reading and writing are not natural processes, our brains are hardwired for communicating through speaking and listening (Hulit, Howard, and Fahey 2018). Researchers and experienced educators can attest to the fact that listening comprehension skills and oral language abilities are generally more developed than students' reading and writing skills, particularly in younger children (Sticht and James 1984). Drawing on the stronger listening comprehension skills of young readers can enhance vocabulary development, grow knowledge of complex language structures, and aid content knowledge as students can comprehend through listening what they would not be able to read. Larger vocabularies and broad content knowledge in turn support reading comprehension and writing skills. As students' reading and writing skills progress, it is important that speaking and listening skills do the same. Speaking is directly connected to our thinking and learning. Opportunities to talk to others about our thoughts require us to be active in our thinking, making decisions about how to explain understanding and reflect on and analyze what we know or may not know. These conversations and discussions can help students make sense of new information and construct new meaning (Barnes and Todd 1995; Halliday 1975). Speaking and listening support the development of all other literacy skills, including reading comprehension and writing, and must be an essential element of effective literacy instruction.

The model promotes literacy instruction that brings together multiple sciences of reading, with the ultimate goal of developing reading, writing, and communication.

> Speaking and listening support the development of all other literacy skills, including reading comprehension and writing, and must be an essential element of effective literacy instruction.

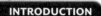

Factors That Contribute to Reading and Writing Success

As mentioned above, success in reading and writing can be influenced by more than just explicit instruction in the components of literacy. Duke and Cartwright's (2021) Active View of Reading points to important factors that impact students, including cultural knowledge, motivation and engagement, and executive functioning skills. Each of these can be a determiner of student success. As well as addressing the needs of those students who are progressing at different rates, differentiation is essential for providing all students with the necessary tools for success. Many students enter our classrooms speaking a language other than English and need extra support while attaining English language proficiency. Below is a discussion of how teachers can create a supportive classroom environment and address these additional factors.

Motivating Students to Read

Ensuring that students are interested and engaged in the work of reading is one aspect of instruction that cannot be overlooked. Teachers must identify a range of ways to both engage and motivate their students.

INTERESTS

> Ensuring that students have access to a wide range of texts will help each student find something to be passionate about.

To foster a lifelong love for reading and writing that extends beyond the day-to-day literacy tasks of classroom life, teachers should become familiar with students' interests as early in the school year as possible with the goal of providing students with reading materials and writing assignments that are tailored to their interests, passions, and wonderings. Ensuring that students have access to a wide range of texts will help each student find something to be passionate about. Providing suggestions rather than rules about the types of texts to read allows for students to choose books that are informational, or contain poetry, or fables, or stories. Once these high-interest texts and assignments are made available, students are more likely to be self-motivated to read and write because they want to discover and share more about the topics that interest them. This self-motivated act of reading and writing develops students' desire to learn that is so important in accessing content from a wide range of texts and text types beyond their interests. Reading and writing about texts of interest allows students to fine-tune their skills in the context of experiences that are interesting, familiar, and comfortable for them, in turn providing them with the confidence and practice needed to effectively navigate texts that are more advanced, unfamiliar, or unexciting.

AUTHENTIC OPPORTUNITIES

There are several ways to offer authentic opportunities for students to purposefully engage with interesting texts. Challenge students to use reading to solve a problem, research something of interest, or compare characters they fall in love with. Reading challenges such as these can be formulated and scripted by the teacher or they can be generic and allow for students to both create the pathway and discover the journey. For example, if a group of fifth-grade students shows interest in the civil rights movement after a social studies lesson, provide a text set for them to engage with. Have students choose which texts to read, which pathway to follow, and how they will share what they have learned. Similarly, if a group of third graders shows interest in a character, put together a bin of texts with similar characters. Provide students with the challenge: discover who is most interesting and prove it. These types of opportunities increase student time spent reading and writing. Without motivation, students will spend less time reading and writing, providing less opportunity to perfect literacy skills, build knowledge, and develop wide vocabulary.

OUTSIDE READING

In addition to discovering students' interests and providing suggestions and texts based on your findings, one of the easiest and most effective ways to improve reading comprehension and writing ability is to promote extensive reading outside of class. Students who frequently read a wide variety of materials have better vocabularies and better reading comprehension skills. They also can use those texts as models for future writing. As Randall Ryder and Michael Graves (2003) point out, wide reading fosters automaticity in students because it exposes them to more words in different contexts, provides them with knowledge on a variety of topics, and promotes lifelong reading habits.

A teacher's attitude toward reading and writing, especially for pleasure outside of school, has a tremendous effect on students in the classroom. Teachers who talk enthusiastically about books they have read and who model reading and writing as enjoyable and fulfilling experiences foster a love for reading and writing in their students. Teachers who can recommend books that are particularly engaging and interesting can increase student motivation tremendously. Teachers should have an intimate knowledge of reading materials for a wide range of abilities so they can recommend books to any student to read outside of class.

> Teachers who talk enthusiastically about books they have read and who model reading and writing as enjoyable, fulfilling experiences foster a love for reading and writing in their students.

THE CLASSROOM LIBRARY

A powerful step is to set up a classroom library. Why is it important to have a classroom library? According to Lesley Mandel Morrow (2003), children in classrooms with book collections read 50 percent more books than children in classrooms without such collections.

Teachers can collaborate with the school librarian or media specialist and parent organizations to build a sizeable collection of texts, which should be a mixture of fiction and nonfiction. Bear in mind that this library may serve to generate the interest to read about many different subjects, so providing students with a wide range of texts from which to choose will be beneficial in fostering their desire and motivation to read and write. Be sure to provide texts that are at your students' readiness levels along with texts that may present more of a challenge. Students can build their prior knowledge about a given topic at a less challenging reading level, preparing them to apply a variety of reading strategies to navigate more advanced texts on the same topic. Michael Pressley and his colleagues (2003) found that high-motivation and high-performing classrooms were, above all, filled with books at different levels of text difficulty.

The reading materials should be housed in bookcases that provide easy access for students to browse and choose books. Use tubs to hold magazines and articles on related topics and themes. Students will be better able to incorporate their new learning through independent reading into their existing prior knowledge if the materials are purposefully organized: science, science fiction, history, historical fiction, mystery, fantasy, adventure, and other types of literature.

> While we can entice students with carefully crafted libraries, success may still be hindered if we neglect to address their individual needs.

Once the materials are in place, create opportunities to incorporate them into your instruction. Assign projects and writing assignments that require students to use the classroom library materials to independently learn more about different topics. Also encourage wide reading by making independent and accountable reading a regular classroom activity. If students are not doing any reading outside of school, school should provide some time for students to read in class. It may be nearly impossible to imagine blocking out any time for silent reading in today's demanding classrooms, but as Stephen Krashen (2009) makes clear in his "81 Generalizations about Free Voluntary Reading," more reading leads to better reading, faster reading, better writing, more writing, and better language acquisition for English learners.

Motivation is one factor that impacts the successful development of reading and writing ability. While we can entice students with carefully crafted libraries, success may still be hindered if we neglect to address their individual needs. This means meeting students where they are and providing appropriate instruction and support, whether they are an English learner, striving reader, or accelerated learner.

Differentiation

As teachers, we know that students come into our classrooms at varying reading, writing, and readiness levels to access the content at hand. Each strategy in this book offers suggestions for differentiating for various groups of students so that they can benefit from the strategy, whether those groups are English learners, striving (below grade level), or accelerated (above grade level) students. All students in our classrooms deserve access to rich and rigorous content. Differentiating the content, the process, the product, and the environment allows for all students to find success in learning to read and write.

> Differentiating the content, the process, the product, and the environment allows for all students to find success in learning to read and write.

Our goal is to help students acquire proficiency in reading and writing. As part of this goal, it is our responsibility to provide students with meaningful and interesting contexts to learn language and build their reading and writing skills. In doing so, teachers simultaneously aid in the development of students' collaborative, communicative, and group-based skills emphasized in speaking and listening standards, subsequently helping all students to strategically communicate and interact with those around them within the context of the English language.

English Learners

When implementing the strategies in this book, discuss with students the importance of using a variety of strategies to understand and write about the new information that they glean from text. This helps students understand the importance of developing finely tuned reading and writing skills. The explicit instruction of these reading and writing strategies provides all learners with meaningful contexts for learning language, so this discussion is necessary for establishing a reason for reading and writing, not only for your English language learners, but for all of your students. Providing English learners with scaffolds for accessing content, developing literacy skills, and engaging with the context of unfamiliar cultural references builds pathways for students to find success. Giving English learners access to texts that will help develop their overall reading abilities is also essential to developing their writing skills. Ample opportunities to engage with rich content support multilingual students in developing the knowledge and vocabulary that underpins their understanding. In addition, English learners "will benefit from actively seeking exposure to language and social interaction with others who can provide meaningful input in the

second language. Furthermore, they—and you, the teacher—can enhance students' English language skills by placing language learning in meaningful and interesting contexts" (Dunlap and Weisman 2006, 11).

Striving Learners

In addition to building motivation through interest-based texts, striving students will benefit from scaffolding. While all students benefit from explicit, authentic instruction, these are crucial elements for striving readers. Striving readers can benefit from participating in a small group before the whole-class lesson, which gives them the opportunity to learn the information in a lower-risk environment with text at a developmentally appropriate level. They may also need further practice with the content after instruction. It is vital that striving learners are provided with additional scaffolds to ensure their success.

Accelerated Learners

While it is critical to differentiate lessons for the striving learner, accelerated students also benefit from modifications to instruction. Teachers can challenge accelerated learners by extending the content either in depth or breadth (Tomlinson 2014). In addition, teachers can provide accelerated learners with opportunities to demonstrate their understanding of content by modifying the process (how students are provided the content) or the product (what students produce to demonstrate understanding). Adapting curriculum for accelerated learners also addresses issues of motivation, as providing tasks that are cognitively challenging maintains their interest.

Flexible Grouping

Throughout this text, we recommend ways to differentiate the lessons to better accommodate all students. Some modalities we recommend are whole class, small groups, collaborative learning, and partner pairs.

Whole class may be used for:

- introducing a new strategy
- modeling think-alouds to show students how to use the strategy
- practicing think-alouds and allowing students to share their experiences and ideas using the strategy

Small groups may be used for:

- pre-teaching new strategies and vocabulary to English learners or striving students
- providing more intensive instruction for striving students

- checking students' understanding of how to apply strategies to the text they are reading or composing
- introducing accelerated students to a strategy so that they can apply it independently to more challenging texts
- encouraging students to use a strategy to think more deeply than they might have imagined possible

Collaborative learning may be used for:

- allowing students to practice strategies without teacher involvement (the teacher is available and "walking the room" to monitor group progress and understanding)
- providing striving students with peer support in completing tasks (when groups are strategically formed)

Pair students with partners to:

- strategically scaffold and support their learning (e.g., pair a striving student with a "near-peer"—someone who is just ahead of their partner)
- share responses and ideas when trying out strategies

Cultural Relevance

Students learn best when they feel they can take risks and be open to new experiences. For this to happen, teachers need to create spaces where everyone feels valued and that they belong. One way to do this is to design a classroom that represents the diverse backgrounds and cultures of our students. Being mindful of students' home lives, cultures, and language experiences is known as being culturally and linguistically responsive. According to Sharroky Hollie, cultural and linguistic responsiveness (CLR) can be defined as the "validation and affirmation of the home (indigenous) culture and home language for the purposes of building and bridging the student to success in the culture of academia and mainstream society" (2018, 23).

Being a culturally and linguistically responsive educator is a journey. The concepts may be well-known, or they may be new. Culturally and linguistically responsive educators are self-aware and socially aware. They are aware of their own cultural backgrounds, which include ethnicity, nationality, religion, age, and gender, among other things. In the classroom, culturally and linguistically responsive educators are sensitive to cultural differences and have an unconditional positive regard for students and their cultures. They strive to continually learn

> In the classroom, culturally and linguistically responsive educators are sensitive to cultural differences and have an unconditional positive regard for students and their cultures.

about students and their cultures, adjusting their perspectives and practices to best serve students.

Culturally and linguistically responsive classrooms are print-rich and display the linguistic supports multilingual learners and others need to be successful. This includes the academic vocabulary that students are learning, which they need to access to be able to discuss language and content. In addition, these classrooms are active. Students utilize the four language components and are engaged in discussions with peers and teachers. They are physically active and move around the room to work with peers on a variety of projects. The materials being utilized reflect a variety of cultures and perspectives, and student work is prominently displayed and honored.

Culturally and linguistically responsive educators design curriculum by selecting texts with characters and pictures that represent their students. They create shared writing pieces that draw from the students' home languages and cultures. They encourage students to research areas of interest and produce art that validates and exhibits their cultures. Culturally and linguistically responsive educators are constantly reevaluating their curricular choices to ensure all students are represented and validated.

Hollie (2018) embraces a philosophy of affirming students' home cultures and languages and suggests educators "love outrageously." To be culturally and linguistically responsive, educators must know their students. When educators validate students' cultures and languages through classroom management and materials, they help students see themselves reflected in the curriculum and allow students to use their backgrounds to supplement the classroom learning environment.

> Culturally and linguistically responsive educators design curriculum by selecting texts with characters and pictures that represent their students.

Taking a culturally and linguistically responsive stance is a holistic approach. It embraces the whole learner. When students feel they belong, are validated, and are represented in the curriculum, they are open and connected to the learning. Teaching in this manner allows for everyone's story to be told.

How to Use This Book

This book includes a variety of strategies that can be integrated into any language arts curriculum to improve students' reading and writing skills: promoting word consciousness, analyzing word parts, activating and developing knowledge through vocabulary development and content learning, using think-alouds and monitoring comprehension, questioning, summarizing, using visual representations and mental imagery, using text structure and text features, incorporating mentor text, using graphic organizers, and modeling writing. These research-based instructional strategies will help teachers bridge the gap between the science of literacy instruction and classroom practice.

The strategies are presented in three sections: I) Word Recognition; II) Reading Comprehension and Content Knowledge; and III) Writing. These three sections correspond with three professional resources: *What the Science of Reading Says about Word Recognition* (Jump and Johnson 2023), *What the Science of Reading Says about Comprehension and Content Knowledge* (Jump and Kopp 2023), and *What the Science of Reading Says about Writing* (Jump and Wolfe 2023).

Each section opens with an overview of research in that area to emphasize the importance of that particular component. There is a clear and detailed explanation of the component, suggestions for instruction, and best practices. This information provides teachers with the solid foundation of knowledge to provide deeper, more meaningful instruction to their students.

Following each overview are a variety of instructional strategies to improve students' reading and writing. The strategies in the book include the following:

- background information that includes a description and purpose of the strategy and the research basis for the strategy
- the objective of the strategy
- a detailed description of how to implement the strategy, including any special preparation that might be needed
- suggestions for differentiating instruction

When applicable, the strategy includes one or more activity sheets as reproducibles in this book and in the digital resources. Grade-level examples of how the strategy is applied are also included when applicable. For more information about the digital resources, see page 180.

SECTION I:

Word Recognition

The strategies in this section correspond with key competencies identified in *What the Science of Reading Says about Word Recognition* (Jump and Johnson 2023). These research-based instructional strategies will help teachers bridge the gap between the science of literacy instruction and classroom practice.

Strategy	Skills and Understandings Addressed				
	Phonological Awareness	Phonics	Beyond Foundational Phonics	Sight Word Automaticity	Fluency
Elkonin Boxes	■				
What Do I See?	■				
Word Challenge		■			
Word Ladders		■			
Word Sort		■			
Scrambled Words		■			
Making Words Tree			■		
Word Part Detective			■		

Strategy	Skills and Understandings Addressed *(cont.)*				
	Phonological Awareness	Phonics	Beyond Foundational Phonics	Sight Word Automaticity	Fluency
Shades of Meaning			■		
Sight Word Bingo				■	
Heart Words/Letters				■	
Word Show				■	
Making Phrases					■
Punctuation Matters!					■

Word Recognition

Before children even enter a classroom, they have begun to build aspects of literacy they will use on the road to becoming lifelong readers. This wealth of knowledge includes concepts of print (print carries meaning), phonological awareness (manipulating units of oral language), and the alphabetic principle (understanding that letters represent sounds). Once children have gained knowledge in these areas, they are ready for instruction in word recognition. The goal of instruction in word recognition is for readers to develop automaticity with words, allowing their cognitive focus to shift to meaning making (Scarborough 2001). Word recognition includes instruction in phonics (the study of speech sounds related to reading), decoding (using understanding of letter-sound relationships to decipher a word), encoding (using decoding knowledge to produce letter patterns when spelling), sight recognition (words recognized immediately, often consisting of high-frequency words), and fluency (reading with accuracy, pacing, and expression).

It can be helpful to turn to Ehri's (1987; 1992; 2005; 2020) phases of word reading to better understand the development of word recognition skills. Ehri describes four overlapping phases of word reading that students move through as they learn to read (decode) and spell (encode). Each phase is labeled to reflect and describe the type of knowledge applied during it to read and spell words: pre-alphabetic, partial alphabetic, full alphabetic, and consolidated alphabetic (Ehri 1987; 1992; 1998; 2020). The chart below summarizes readers' skills in each phase.

Phase of Word Reading	Skills
Pre-Alphabetic	Early readers apply visual, nonalphabetic cues to read words. For example, remembering the "two round eyes" for the *oo* in *look* (Ehri 1998), the tail at the end of *dog*, or the hump in the middle of *camel* (Gough, Juel, and Roper-Schneider 1983).
Partial Alphabetic	Learners apply beginning knowledge of letter-sound correspondence to reading words, often focusing on the initial and the final consonants. For example, remembering /s/ and /n/ to read *spoon* (Ehri 1998). Readers often combine this knowledge with context clues to recognize words. They are often better able to recognize the words in context than in isolation.
Full Alphabetic	Readers have a well-developed knowledge of letter-sound correspondence. They use decoding skills to analyze letter-sound connections within words to read and spell them from memory (Ehri 2020).
Consolidated Alphabetic	Learners consolidate letter patterns into larger patterns that represent syllables and morphemes, have stored these in memory, and can apply them to decode and make connections to multisyllabic words (Ehri 2020).

Phonological and Phonemic Awareness

At the pre-alphabetic stage, both phonological and phonemic awareness rely completely on oral language and the detection of sounds. Phonological awareness is broader than phonemic awareness and includes manipulating units of oral language, for instance, identifying individual words in a sentence, separating syllables in a word, separating the sounds in a word, and determining beginning, medial, and ending sounds in a word. While there are twenty-six letters in the English alphabet, there are forty-four phonemes in the language, because some sounds are represented by more than one letter, such as /sh/. For readers to move to the word recognition stage, it is crucial for them to gain a strong foundation in phonemic awareness (Adams 2011; Ehri 2014, 2020; Ehri et al. 2001). Phonemic awareness specifically relates to the manipulation of the individual sounds in a word. Adams (2011, 14) shares six tasks recommended by the National Reading Panel (2000) in building phonemic awareness:

1. Phoneme isolation: "Tell me the first sound in the word *paste*." (/p/)

2. Phoneme identity: "Tell me the sound that is the same in the words *bike*, *boy*, and *bell*." (/b/)

3. Phoneme categorization: "Which word does not belong: *bus*, *bun*, or *rug*?" (*rug*)

4. Phoneme blending: "What word is /s/ /t/ /o/ /p/?" (*stop*)

5. Phoneme segmentation: "How many sounds are there in *ship*?" (three: /sh/ /i/ /p/)

6. Phoneme deletion: "What word is *smile* without the /s/?" (*mile*)

For instance, in a phonemic awareness activity, a teacher might provide the word *bat* and ask the student to orally separate the word into its individual sounds: /b/ /a/ /t/. Some activities that support the acquisition of phonemic awareness are rhyme and alliteration, orally tapping out syllables in words, manipulating onsets and rimes (cat, mat, sat, hat), and identifying and matching initial, medial, and final sounds (Which picture shows something that begins with /s/? Which shows something that ends with /s/?).

> Phonological awareness is broader than phonemic awareness and includes manipulating units of oral language, for instance, identifying individual words in a sentence, separating syllables in a word, separating the sounds in a word, and determining beginning, medial, and ending sounds in a word.

Phonics

Phonics instruction is teaching the relationships between sounds (phonemes) and letters (graphemes). The research is clear that children benefit from systematic (following a scope and sequence) and explicit instruction (direct teaching) in phonics (Ehri et al. 2001; Ehri 2020; National Early Literacy Panel

2008; NRP 2000; Snow and Juel 2005; Wanzek et al. 2018). Teachers provide early readers with systematic instruction by sequencing skills from simple to complex, e.g., starting with beginning sounds since they are easiest to recognize. Teachers provide early readers with explicit instruction on how to match a letter to the sound or sounds (phonemes) it represents, e.g., the letter *g* can make two sounds. Sometimes it is a hard sound like the *g* in *dig*, and sometimes it is a soft sound like the *g* in *gem*. It can be useful to introduce high-utility sounds/spellings first (e.g., /ă/, *a*; /m/, *m*; /t/, *t*) so students can begin to blend letters in words and move through the phases. It is also important for words to be practiced in context so students can cement the syntactic and semantic correspondence of those words (Ehri 2020). This consistent practice leads to the building of a sight-word bank that readers can use when encountering text.

Decoding and Encoding

Decoding and encoding have a reciprocal relationship. While decoding is taking the sounds off the page to read words, encoding (spelling) is the production of letters to represent sounds. Allowing children in the pre-alphabetic and the partial alphabetic stages to write using invented spelling can be a valuable literacy strategy (Adams 2011). For instance, encouraging young readers to sound out words as they spell them reinforces matching letters to sounds (e.g., /k/ /ă/ /t/ *cat*). This in turn builds their phonics knowledge. The same grapheme-phoneme relationships readers rely on for word recognition in reading are called upon for spelling. Spelling patterns can also be referred to as *orthography* (Ehri 2020). Readers' ability to accurately map letters and letter combinations to sounds and store these in memory (a process referred to as *orthographic mapping*) is crucial to spelling development. Knowledge of words and word parts is essential to reading and spelling, and readers must be able to apply this knowledge accurately and efficiently. This process of studying words and word parts is known as *word study* (Bear et al. 2020). An integrated word study approach as described in this section provides opportunities for the development of orthographic knowledge alongside the application of such word study to reading. Young readers will also encounter unknown words when encoding (spelling) a word either mentally (e.g., when looking something up) or physically (when writing). It is unlikely that memorizing the spelling of thousands of words is efficient, or even possible, so it makes sense to be strategic. Effective spelling instruction is explicit about and takes advantage of the relationships between how words look, how they sound, and what they mean, integrating and enhancing readers' existing decoding knowledge and building strategies for word analysis.

> Knowledge of words and word parts is essential to reading and spelling, and readers must be able to apply this knowledge accurately and efficiently.

What do we do when we encounter unknown words? How do we apply our knowledge? The research tells us that as readers advance to the consolidated alphabetic stage, they will strategically apply knowledge of morphemes (the smallest grammatical unit that carries meaning, such as *re–*, *–ing*, *–ed*) to decode unfamiliar multisyllabic words (Bhattacharya and Ehri 2004; Shefelbine and Calhoun 1991). "Through this process, as the connections between spelling, sound, and meaning become completely and reliably represented and bound together, the word will become readable at a glance, it will become a 'sight word'" (Adams 2011, 17).

Sight Word Automaticity

For readers to advance through the phases, it is crucial that they build a sight-word bank. Sight words are words readers know automatically, without having to sound them out (sometimes referred to as *automaticity*). These sight words include high-frequency words, those words that occur most frequently in the English language. However, a reader's sight-word bank consists of more than just high-frequency words. It includes any words the reader knows on sight. Most words are phonetically decodable; however, there are some words that are irregular, for instance, *of* /uv/ and *as* /az/. It can be helpful for readers to be taught these words explicitly, as they don't lend themselves to a decoding strategy (Ehri 2014). Continued, repeated exposure to words through explicit instruction and word play is a must to build automaticity. Word study instruction should be planned in ways that foster automaticity and continue to build word reading skills in and out of context.

Fluency

A large sight-word bank coupled with decoding skills can lead students to becoming fluent readers. Fluency is the ability to read fluidly. Fluent reading has three aspects—accuracy, pacing, and expression. When fluent readers read aloud, their reading is accurate, at a quick but natural pace, and has expression. When fluent readers read silently, reading is highly automatic, with readers grouping words together for meaning rather than reading word by word. When readers attain an appropriate level of fluency, they can dedicate their attention to comprehension. Instruction that builds decoding skills and automaticity supports fluency. Additional explicit instruction and practice in pace, proper expression, vocabulary, and language structures (discussed later in this book) aid the development of fluent readers. Attention to accuracy and automaticity is important, however, we should not focus exclusively on reading rate (accurate word count per minute) as an indicator of fluency. In fact, one characteristic of disfluent readers is reading text excessively fast, ignoring punctuation. When students attend to punctuation and read

> When readers attain an appropriate level of fluency, they can dedicate their attention to comprehension.

with expression, this can indicate comprehension; therefore fluency instruction and practice should consider all three elements of fluency. Wide reading, increasing volume (amount) of reading, modeling of fluent reading, opportunities to demonstrate expression, and repeated and assisted reading are all strategies shown to support fluency (Rasinski et al. 2017).

Putting It All Together

Teachers of early readers have a huge responsibility, assisting students in moving through the phases of word reading. The development of phonemic awareness and strong orthographic representations paves the way for quick, accurate decoding and encoding, freeing up resources for comprehension and expression. Word study that integrates decoding and encoding instruction with opportunities to engage in fluency practice is essential for continued development of word recognition skills.

Elkonin Boxes

Objectives

- Isolate and pronounce initial, medial vowel, and final sounds (phonemes) in spoken single-syllable words.

Background Information

Phonemic awareness practice provides early readers with opportunities to manipulate language. The goal of Elkonin Boxes is to strengthen emergent readers' ability to isolate initial, medial vowel, and final sounds when given a whole word by the teacher (Keesey, Konrad, and Joseph 2015). Oral language manipulation is essential for emergent readers to become aware that whole words consist of individual sounds. Begin by using words with two phonemes and increase the difficulty by progressing to words with three and four phonemes.

Materials

- *Elkonin Boxes* (select from pages 27–29)
- tokens (2–4 per student)

Process

1. Identify words to use for practice (see lists on page 26).
2. Give each student an *Elkonin Boxes* activity sheet and tokens. Have students place the tokens in the circles below the boxes.
3. State a target word for students to segment (e.g., *am*).
4. Have students say each sound (phoneme) aloud while pushing a token up into the box to indicate the phoneme—/a/ /m/.
5. If students are ready, ask them to write the letters that make the sounds below the boxes.

Differentiation

Provide a small mirror for students who have a hard time hearing individual sounds. Slowly segment a two-phoneme word, making exaggerated motions with your mouth as you produce each sound. Ask students to repeat the sounds you made and look in their mirrors to see their mouths move as they make each sound. Do this with a few words before having them try with the Elkonin boxes. Students can slowly move counters as they look in their mirrors to see their mouths move with each sound that they make.

Beginners should start with the two-box activity sheet. More advanced students can be given activity sheets with three or four boxes and can be asked to write the letters that represent the sounds on their activity sheets. To develop students' vocabulary, consider providing picture cards for the words students will segment.

Practice Words

Words with Two Phonemes/Sounds					
am	as	if	is	of	up
an	at	in	it	on	us

Words with Three Phonemes/Sounds					
bat	cat	fun	map	rot	tug
bed	cup	get	met	run	van
big	cut	him	pen	sad	vet
bug	fed	hot	pig	sun	web
can	fit	let	rip	top	wig

Words with Four Phonemes/Sounds					
bump	dent	flip	last	plug	stop
clam	drip	frog	left	rest	swan
clap	drum	glad	lift	sand	swim
clip	felt	grab	past	sled	vest
cost	flag	hand	plan	stem	wilt

Name: _____ Date: _____

Elkonin Boxes: Two Sounds

Directions: Listen to your teacher. Say the sounds and push the counters into the boxes.

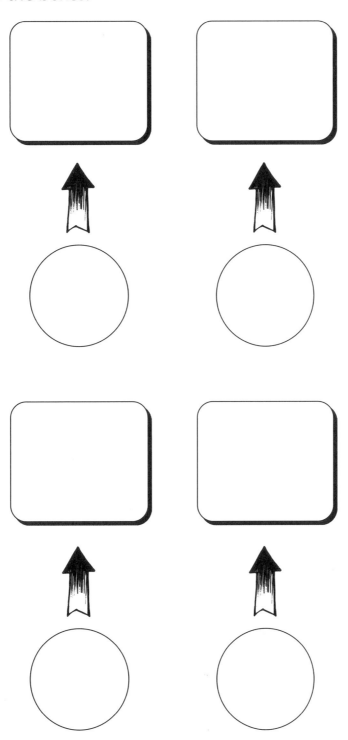

Elkonin Boxes: Three Sounds

Directions: Listen to your teacher. Say the sounds and push the counters into the boxes.

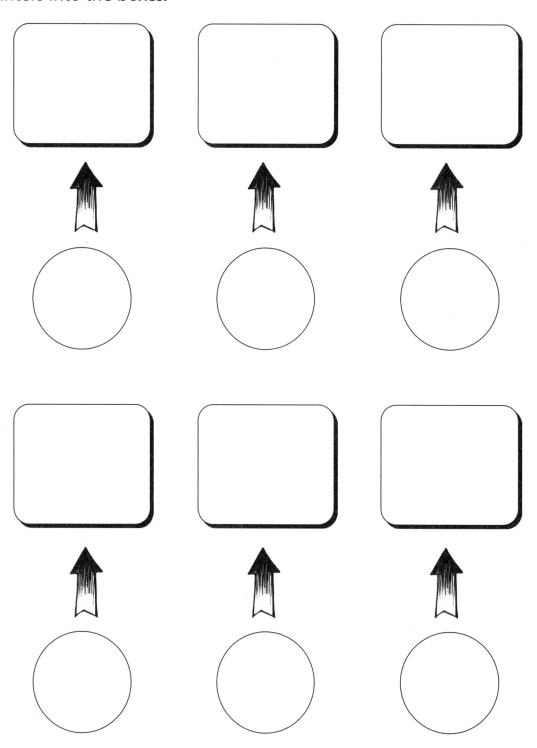

Name: _____ Date: _____

Elkonin Boxes: Four Sounds

Directions: Listen to your teacher. Say the sounds and push the counters into the boxes.

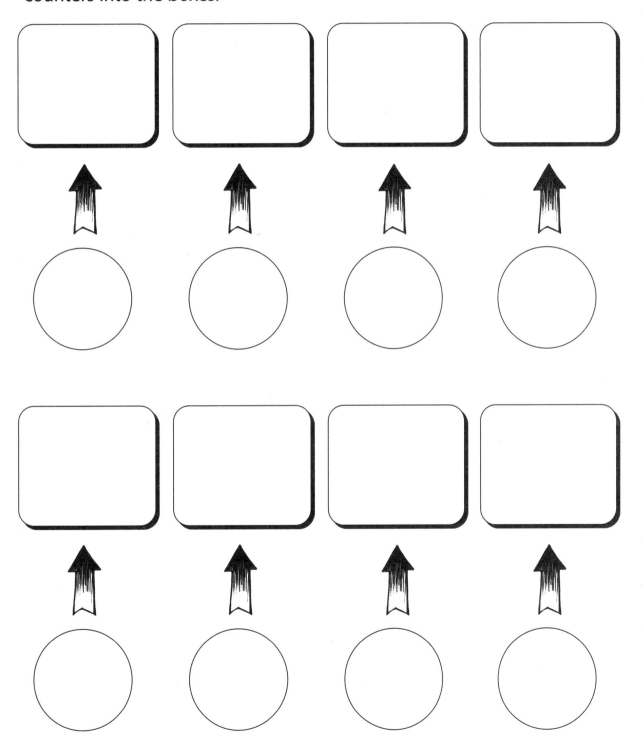

What Do I See?

Objectives

- Orally blend and segment sounds (phonemes) of single-syllable spoken words.

Background Information

Phonological and phonemic awareness develop step by step. Students move from hearing individual words in sentences to identifying each word in a compound word to counting syllables in words. The goal of What Do I See? is for emergent readers to orally blend sounds to produce the name of an item that the teacher has identified. Ultimately, we want students to hear and manipulate individual sounds in words. Students need practice to hear a word and segment it into its individual sounds. They need many opportunities to practice blending sounds into a word.

Materials

- *What Do I See? Picture Cards* (pages 32–34)

Process

1. Cut apart and display the *What Do I See? Picture Cards*.

2. Choose one of the images to be the mystery picture, for example, *map*. Read the poem below and for the last line, orally segment the word by separating it into individual sounds. For *map*, segment like this: /m/ /ă/ /p/.

   What do I see?
   What can it be?
   Listen, listen,
   Listen to me
   I see a _____ (segmented word).

3. Have students repeat the sounds you made, blending them together and determining the word is *map*. Ask them to point to the picture of the map.

4. Continue the activity with other words.

5. Have students practice with partners. Be sure at least one in the pair can independently segment words.

6. Ask the partner who can segment to select a mystery picture and say the rhyme, segmenting the word for the last line.

7. Have the child listening repeat the sounds, blend, and point to the picture of the segmented word.

Differentiation

Before the Lesson: Ensure English language learners know the name of each picture.

During the Lesson: Select words to segment and blend based on student ability. The *What Do I See? Picture Cards* include pictures of words with three phonemes (pen, mop, fan, box, bell, cat, pig, bat, can) and pictures of words with four phonemes (brush, desk, slide, clock, flag, frog, sled, plug, clip). An alternate activity is to identify actual items in the classroom and use them as mystery items.

What Do I See? Picture Cards

What Do I See? Picture Cards *(cont.)*

What Do I See? Picture Cards *(cont.)*

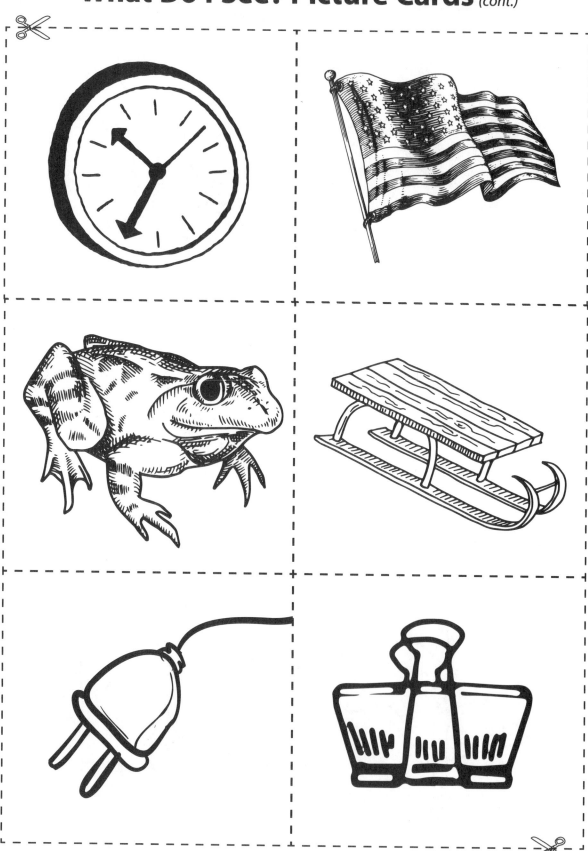

Word Challenge

Objectives

- Know and apply grade-level phonics and word analysis skills in decoding words both in isolation and in text.

Background Information

Manipulating the parts of words with the same rime (*can, pan, man,* and *ran*) allows readers to play with vowels in a supported way, as the vowel is presented as a chunk (Goswami 2008). This manipulation consists of partnering onsets (the initial phonological sound) with rimes (everything in the syllable after the initial sound). Studying these words is useful, since thirty-seven rimes can be used to generate five hundred different words (Wylie and Durrell 1970). When introducing these words, it makes sense to begin with consonant-vowel-consonant (CVC) words (e.g., *cat, mat, sat*). Once students have learned the phonics skill that supports the rime (e.g., short *a* for *–an*), this type of practice builds automaticity. After being introduced to consonant blends (e.g., *bl, cl, tr*), readers can use them to create new words with the rimes (e.g., *black, flack, track*).

Materials

- *Word Challenge* (page 37)
- timer

Process

1. Decide if you want students to complete the challenge as individuals, in pairs, or in small groups.

2. Select a rime (see the list on page 36), and write it at the top of the *Word Challenge* activity sheet (e.g., *at*). Make one copy for each student (or group).

3. Demonstrate to the whole group how to make words with rimes. Write a rime on the board and ask students to name words that can be made with that rime. List the words on the board.

4. Distribute *Word Challenge* to students. Have them identify the rime (e.g., *at*) at the top of the page. Tell students you are going to give them a certain amount of time to list as many words with that rime as they can.

5. Start the timer, and have students write their words (e.g., *cat, bat, mat, rat, sat, hat, pat*). When time is up, have students count the number of words they created and read their list to the group.

6. As an extension, allow students to create nonsense words using the rime as well as actual words (e.g., *lat, crat, frat*). Have students tell whether each word is a nonsense word or a real word.

Differentiation

Introduce each rime individually prior to the activity. Carefully determine group size and members to support and challenge students as needed. Select short vowel rimes for beginning readers and rimes with long vowel sounds for those who are more advanced.

Common Rimes

These thirty-seven common rimes can be used to play the game. They can be used to form five hundred primary words (Wylie and Durrell 1970).

ack	ail	ain	ake	ale	ame
an	ank	ap	ash	at	ate
aw	ay	eat	ell	est	ice
ick	ide	ight	ill	in	ine
ing	ink	ip	ir	ock	oke
op	or	ore	uck	ug	ump
unk					

Name: _____ Date: _____

Word Challenge

Directions: Look at the word part. Write words with the word part.
Think of as many as you can.

Word part:

_____   _____

_____   _____

_____   _____

_____   _____

_____   _____

_____   _____

_____   _____

_____   _____

Word Ladders

Objectives

- Know and apply grade-level phonics and word analysis skills in decoding words both in isolation and in text.

Background Information

When acquiring strong phonics skills, students need opportunities to play with the sounds within words (Adams 1994; Bear et al. 2020). With Word Ladders, students use their analytical letter-sound skills to build new words. This reinforces their knowledge of initial, medial, and final sounds/spellings. Students begin with a word on the bottom rung of the ladder and manipulate individual phonemes and graphemes within the word to generate new words until they reach the top rung of the ladder.

Materials

- list of six words (see Word Ladder Words, page 39)
- *Three-Letter Word Ladder, Four-Letter Word Ladder*, or *Five-Letter Word Ladder* (pages 41–43)

Process

1. Determine whether students will use three-letter, four-letter, or five-letter words, and make copies of the corresponding activity sheet.

2. Distribute the activity sheets. Provide the start word, and have students write it on the bottom rung.

3. Say the next word. Have students determine which sound changes and write the word on the next rung up on the ladder (e.g., bottom rung: *pen*, next rung: *pet*).

4. Continue naming words and having students write them until the top of the ladder is reached.

5. Have students practice reading each word on the word ladder.

Differentiation

Scaffold the process by working together to complete the ladder as a whole class or in a small group. Write the letter that stays the same on the spaces and let students identify the letter that changes.

Word Ladder Words

Lists for Three-Letter Word Ladders (short vowels)

6. pig	6. cot	6. pit	6. cut	6. lot
5. pit	5. pot	5. pet	5. put	5. log
4. pet	4. pet	4. pot	4. pat	4. fog
3. pot	3. pit	3. rot	3. pot	3. dog
2. cot	2. fit	2. rod	2. dot	2. dig
1. cat	1. fin	1. red	1. dog	1. big

Lists for Four-Letter Word Ladders (long vowels)

6. fine	6. mole	6. mice	6. foal	6. mope
5. pine	5. mile	5. rice	5. coal	5. mode
4. pipe	4. pile	4. ride	4. coat	4. rode
3. ripe	3. file	3. rode	3. moat	3. rude
2. rope	2. fine	2. mode	2. boat	2. rule
1. pope	1. line	1. made	1. beat	1. mule

Lists for Five-Letter Word Ladders (short and long vowels)

6. gross	6. creed	6. seals	6. stump
5. grass	5. creep	5. sears	5. slump
4. grays	4. cheep	4. stars	4. clump
3. plays	3. cheap	3. stare	3. chump
2. plans	2. cheat	2. store	2. chomp
1. plane	1. wheat	1. stone	1. champ

Word Ladder Example

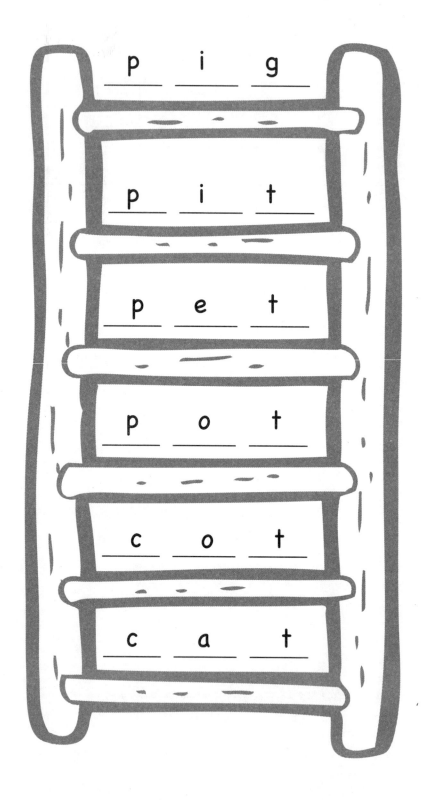

Three-Letter Word Ladder

Directions: Write the start word at the bottom. Change one letter to make a new word. Write the new word on the next step. Climb the ladder.

Name: _____ Date: _____

Four-Letter Word Ladder

Directions: Write the start word at the bottom. Change one letter to make a new word. Write the new word on the next step. Climb the ladder.

Five-Letter Word Ladder

Directions: Write the start word at the bottom. Change one letter to make a new word. Write the new word on the next step. Climb the ladder.

Word Sort

Objectives

- Know and apply grade-level phonics and word analysis skills in decoding words both in isolation and in text.

Background Information

Word Sorts are essentially categorizing words by similarity. The process of categorization requires readers to look closely at words and word parts to find common sound and spelling patterns. In doing so, readers build and reinforce their understandings about the patterns in words to form generalizations that help them make sense of and recognize words. These generalizations aid in decoding, encoding, and fluency building. Donald Bear and colleagues (2020) describe three primary types of Word Sorts: sound, pattern, and meaning sorts. Word Sorts are flexible and can be used to support word recognition skills in whole-group and small-group instruction. This strategy is adapted from the process for a teacher-directed sort (Bear et al. 2020).

Materials

- *Word Sort Cards* (page 47)

Process

1. Determine the words students will use for the activity. Fill in *Word Sort Cards* with the words. Make a copy for each student.

2. Introduce the list of words to students by reading the words aloud. Give special attention to words that may be unfamiliar or difficult to pronounce. Chorally read the words with students.

3. Conduct a think-aloud to establish the categories for sorting. Model asking questions such as "What do I notice about these words?" or "What do some of these words have in common?" Alternately, as students become familiar with Word Sorts, invite them to suggest categories rather than conducting a think-aloud.

4. Record the categories for the Word Sort on chart paper, on a desk or table, or in a word study notebook.

5. Model how to sort a few of the words, checking for student understanding of the sorting criteria. Have students work individually or with partners to sort the rest of the words.

6. Gather students back together to review their sorts. Reflect on the categories and what the words have in common. Reinforce the sorting criteria by asking questions that allow students to verbalize their understanding.

Differentiation

Word Sorts can be made easier or more challenging for small-group instruction. The number of categories for sorting can be increased or decreased, the contrast of the criteria can be made easier or more difficult, and the words chosen for the sort can be more or less complex by the number of spelling patterns addressed. It is common to begin with short vowel sorts (short *a* vs. short *e*) and then progress to short versus long vowel patterns (short *a* vs. long *a*, a_e). Next move to more complex long vowel spellings (e.g., *ai*, *ay*, *eigh*). Then students can move to digraphs (e.g., *sh*, *th*, *wh*, *ch*) and diphthongs (e.g., *aw*, *au*, *oo*, *ew*, *oi*, *oy*, *ow*, *ou*).

The Word Sort criteria can be reinforced throughout the week by conducting "word hunts." Encourage students to record words from their textbooks, trade books, or other reading material. Students can also record words they hear in discussions or encounter in media. At the end of the week, put students in groups or pairs to share the words they found.

Word Sort *Example*

Short a

pan

man

can

fan

cap

map

Short i

pig

pit

wig

fit

dig

sit

Word Sort Cards

Directions: Cut out the cards. Sort the words. Label the groups.

Scrambled Words

Objectives

- Know and apply grade-level phonics and word analysis skills in decoding words both in isolation and in text.

Background Information

When students decode, they look at a printed word and sound it out sound by sound to determine the whole word. When students encode, they are doing the reverse—going letter by letter to build or spell the word. Scrambled Words is a way students can demonstrate their abilities to match sounds (phonemes) to letters (graphemes). It reinforces their knowledge of initial, medial, and final sounds and spellings. Opportunities to play with the sounds in words support the acquisition of strong phonics skills (Adams 1994; Bear et al. 2020).

Materials

- *Scrambled Words Mat* (select from pages 49–51)

Process

1. Determine target words that will be used for the activity. Select a *Scrambled Words Mat* that corresponds with the number of letters in the words. Write the letters needed to spell the words in the empty boxes at the bottom of the mat.

2. Distribute copies of the prepared *Scrambled Words Mat*. Have students cut out the letters below the dotted line.

3. Read aloud the first word. Have the students say each sound out loud while they identify and place the letters in the correct positions in the boxes on the word mat.

4. Continue to name words and have students create the new words in the boxes.

Sample Target Words		
Two-letter words am, an, at, in, it, on, up, us	**Three-letter words** bat, bit, bet, pat, pet, pit, pot	**Four-letter words** base, here, bite, hope, cute

Differentiation

Scaffold by helping students "stretch" the word (e.g., /b/ /ă/ /t/), identify the first letter, and place it in the first box. Continue for the remaining letters. As students develop their abilities to encode, they can be given longer and more difficult words.

Scrambled Words Mat for Two-Letter Words

Directions: Cut out the letter cards. Listen to each word. Place the letters in the boxes to spell the word.

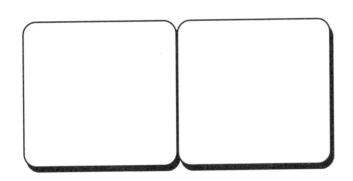

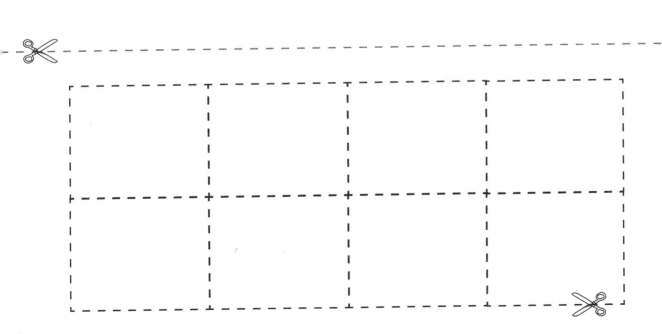

Scrambled Words Mat for
Three-Letter Words

Directions: Cut out the letter cards. Listen to each word. Place the letters in the boxes to spell the word.

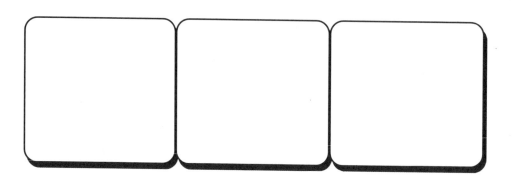

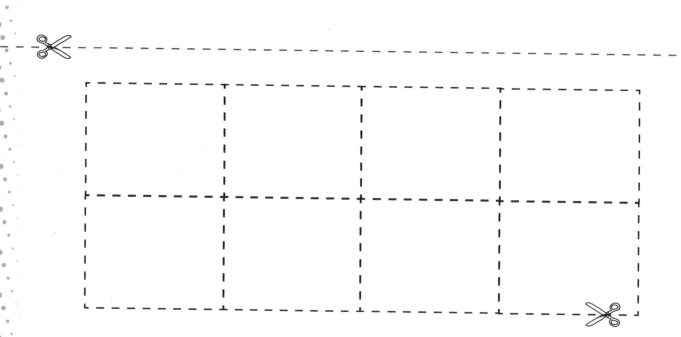

Scrambled Words Mat for Four-Letter Words

Directions: Cut out the letter cards. Listen to each word. Place the letters in the boxes to spell the word.

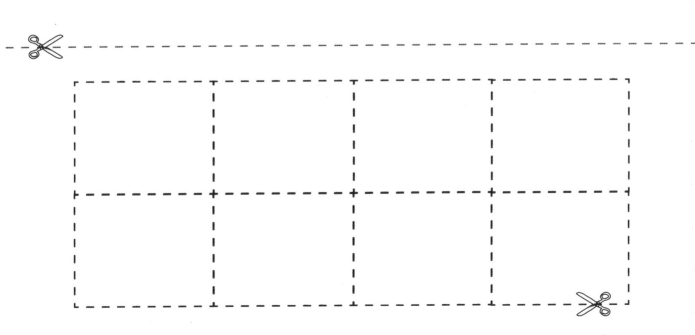

Making Words Tree

Objectives

- Use frequently occurring affixes as clues to the meaning of words.
- Decode words with common prefixes and suffixes.

Background Information

It is estimated that 60 to 80 percent of English words are built by combining bases and affixes (Nagy and Anderson 1984). Words related to specific content areas also have recurring suffixes and bases (Mountain 2015). It is beneficial for students to become familiar with how bases (word parts or stand-alone words) and affixes (prefixes and suffixes) combine to make new words. The Making Words Tree is a graphic organizer that allows students to create new words by adding suffixes to base words. Students then examine how the suffix changes the meaning of the new word. By using suffixes to help determine a word's meaning, students become familiar with frequently occurring word parts. They can use this knowledge to determine the meanings of similar unknown words in other contexts.

Materials

- *Making Words Tree* (page 54)

Process

1. Conduct a mini lesson showing that a *base* carries the basic meaning of a word. A *suffix* is a word part that is added to the end of a base. When a suffix is added to a base, it can change the meaning. Use the word *cat* as an example. Add the suffix *–s*. Discuss how the meaning of the word changed. Other example pairs are *pack + –ed* and *sing + –ing*.

2. Select a suffix and set of words that are appropriate for your students. (See page 53 for examples.) Distribute the *Making Words Tree* activity sheet. Assign the suffix and have students write it at the base of their tree.

3. Provide students with the words orally or on a chart. Have them write the words on their activity sheets and add the suffix to create new words. Students who complete the task before others can be challenged to add the suffix to words they self-select. When students are finished, ask them to read their words to partners.

4. Lead the class in a discussion about how the meaning of the words changed by adding the suffix. Discuss how the sounds of the words changed as well.

Differentiation

Support learners by starting with an easy suffix (–s) and moving on to more difficult suffixes (–ed and –ing). To make this more of a challenge, add words that need to have a final consonant doubled or a final vowel *e* dropped. Another way to advance learning is to discuss how suffixes change the word type. (The suffix –s causes words to change to plural nouns or action verbs. The suffix –ed puts words in the past tense or makes them adjectives. The suffix –ing indicates something is happening right now, i.e., the present tense.)

Suffix	Example Words
–s	shop, car, run, flag, sleep, find, jar
–ed	thank, rest, skill, pass, ask, last, hunt
–ing	brush, mist, sneak, snack, block, toast, land

Making Words Tree

Directions: Write the suffix at the bottom of the tree. Add the suffix to base words. Write the new words.

Word Part Detective

Objectives

- Use frequently occurring affixes as clues to the meaning of a word.
- Determine the meaning of the new word formed when a known prefix is added to a known word (e.g., happy/unhappy, tell/retell).

Background Information

Word Part Detective is a strategy to highlight how words are built using bases and affixes. When students examine words by their parts, they begin to understand that each part holds meaning (Nagy and Scott 2000). Word part analysis can be introduced informally, beginning in kindergarten, when students learn the orthographic patterns of many words. As students progress through the grades, they will encounter hundreds of general and domain-specific words that have bases, prefixes, and suffixes. In first and second grades, students should analyze one or two words per reading selection.

Materials

- *Word Part Detective* (page 57)

Process

1. Distribute copies of *Word Part Detective* to students.

2. Select a prefix or suffix for students to analyze. Have students write the word part at the top of their activity sheets.

3. Guide students through the following steps:

   a. Circle either *prefix* or *suffix*.

   b. Brainstorm words that can be made with the prefix or suffix.

   c. Draw a picture for one of the words.

   d. Create a picture that will help you remember the meaning of the word part.

4. After completing this activity as a whole class, have students work in small groups, with partners, or independently to complete the chart for a different affix.

Differentiation

Scaffold the process by displaying two or three words that have the same prefix (e.g., *unwrap, untie, unhappy*). Ask students how the words are the same and different, and help them identify the prefix and the base words. Discuss how the prefix and base words combine to make new words.

Word Part Detective *Example*

Word part: re

Circle one.	**Meaning:** re– means again
(prefix) suffix	

List five words that contain this word part.

1. redo

2. rewrite

3. replay

4. return

5. recycle

Draw a picture of one of the words from your list.

recycle

Draw something that will help you remember the meaning of this word part.

re = again

Word Part Detective

Directions: Write the word part. Write and draw what it means.

Word part:

Circle one.	Meaning:
prefix suffix	

| List five words that contain this word part.

1._____

2._____

3._____

4._____

5._____ | Draw a picture of one of the words from your list. |

Draw something that will help you remember the meaning of this word part.

Shades of Meaning

Objectives

- Distinguish shades of meaning among verbs that differ in manner and adjectives that differ in intensity by defining them or by acting out the meanings.

- Demonstrate understanding of word relationships and nuances in word meanings.

Background Information

Learning about words and how they relate to other words is an important part of morphology. When students compare words and work to understand their shades of meaning, they gain a deeper and broader understanding of the words (Greenwood and Flanigan 2007). Shades of Meaning presents students with pairs of antonyms and words that are similar to each antonym. Students order the words, using their nuanced meanings as a guide. Students will consider and discuss the shades of meanings of the words and make logical connections.

Materials

- index cards
- *Shaded Meanings* (page 60)

Process

1. Select a row of words from the chart on page 59. You will need the words in set 1 and set 2. Write each word on a separate card.

2. Hold up a word, and ask students to read it. Invite students to share what they think or know about the word. Repeat for all of the words.

3. Explain that some of the words are synonyms, having similar meanings. As a group, sort the cards into synonyms. Next, explain that some of the words are opposites. See if they can identify some of the opposites. As a group, sort the cards into opposites.

4. Next, explain that the words can be thought of as gradients of each other. Words that are gradients have meanings that change slightly from one word to another. Work with the students to sort the words by gradient. Help students select the most extreme word in each set first. Then talk about how the other words relate, and place them in a logical order between the most extreme words. (Example: *terrified, scared, afraid, nervous, brave, adventurous, daring, heroic.*) This activity will generate conversation about what the words mean and how they relate to one another. Students may not agree about how the words should be arranged. However, they should justify their rationale for the order they select.

5. After working with the whole class, give students copies of *Shaded Meanings* and display a different set of words. Support students as they create their own sequences of related words.

6. When students finish, have them discuss their sequences with partners. Finally, work together as a class to see if you can agree on the progression for the assigned words. This activity can be repeated multiple times with different word lists.

Differentiation

To scaffold this activity, you may wish to use fewer words. Provide examples of the words in texts to support understanding. Some students will benefit by seeing picture cues with the words or by acting them out. Another way to support students is to tell them the extreme words that should be written in the first and last boxes on the path. Students can write their assigned words on index cards or sticky notes and order the cards before writing on the activity sheet. Challenge students by inviting them to find their own words and order them by gradient.

Word Gradient Lists

	Set 1	**Set 2**
large/small	large, enormous, massive, gigantic	small, little, tiny, microscopic
sad/happy	sad, unhappy, miserable, gloomy	happy, cheerful, delighted, giddy
afraid/ brave	afraid, scared, terrified, nervous	brave, daring, heroic, adventurous
hot/cold	warm, hot, boiling, blistering	cold, freezing, icy, cool
crawl/walk	stroll, walk, jog, run	crawl, limp, meander, inch
hard/soft	hard, firm, rigid, unbreakable	soft, flexible, fluffy, squishy
heavy/light	heavy, massive, bulky, hulking	light, delicate, fine, feathery
nice/mean	nice, pleasant, delightful, kind	mean, dangerous, evil, rude
loud/quiet	loud, noisy, blaring, deafening	quiet, silent, hushed, faint
light/dark	light, shining, glowing, brilliant	dark, gloomy, unlit, shadowy

Name: _____ **Date:** _____

Shaded Meanings

Directions: Write the words your teacher lists. Try to place the words so the meanings change slightly with each step. Use a crayon to shade the steps from very light to very dark.

Sight Word Bingo

Objectives

- Recognize and read grade-appropriate irregularly spelled words.

Background Information

Sight words are words a reader knows by sight (Ehri 2014). Fluent readers use their large bank of sight words to comprehend text so that their attention can be spent on the content rather than on decoding. There has been much debate on effective ways to teach words so they are recognized by sight. Linnea Ehri (1992, 2005) confirms that words are most effectively stored in memory when a connection is made between the visual and phonetic, in other words, when printed words are said aloud. Ehri termed this *orthographic mapping* (2014). In Sight Word Bingo, students write irregularly spelled words on Bingo grids. Then they listen for the words and mark them, which reinforces orthographic mapping of the words. Repeated, meaningful encounters with words in this manner develops students' sight-word banks.

Materials

- *Sight Word Bingo Game Board* (page 63)

Process

1. Determine the words students will use for the activity. (See page 62 for a list of irregularly spelled words.)

2. Distribute copies of the *Sight Word Bingo Game Board*.

3. Write each word on the board, read it aloud together, and have students write the word in any square on their game boards.

4. Have students read the words on their boards to partners.

5. To play the game, randomly select a word from the list. Read the word aloud and have students say it. Students find the word on their boards and mark it with an *X*.

6. Continue to read words until one of the students has marked four words in a row.

7. After playing the game as a class, students can work with partners to practice reading and marking words.

Differentiation

Write the words on cards, making as many sets as needed for striving students. After you read and show a word, place the card next to the striving student so they can match the words letter by letter. As you write the words on the board, talk about the sounds that are familiar in each word and explain why some parts of the word are irregular.

Sample Words

any	does	of	the	was
are	find	on	their	water
as	from	one	there	were
been	have	or	they	word
come	his	people	to	work
could	is	said	two	would
do	kind	some	want	you

Name: _____ **Date:** _____

Sight Word Bingo Game Board

Directions: Write words in the spaces. Mark an **X** on each word when your teacher says it. Try to get Bingo!

Heart Words/Letters

Objectives

- Recognize and read grade-appropriate irregularly spelled words.
- Identify words with inconsistent but common spelling-sound correspondences.

Background Information

Heart Words/Letters teaches students how to read and spell irregular sight words that are largely undecodable. The irregular letter-sound relationships must be remembered "by heart" (Farrell, Hunter, and Osenga 2019; Fessel and Kennedy 2019). The strategy is used with high-frequency words that need to be read and spelled automatically, such as *are*, *have*, *some*, and *should*. Heart Words helps students recognize and identify the parts of words that are decodable and the parts that are irregular. The goal is for these words to become sight words that can be read automatically.

Materials

- *Heart Words Record Sheet* (page 66)

Process

1. Select the Heart Words that will be taught. Some examples are in the chart on page 65.

2. Distribute *Heart Words Record Sheet* to students.

3. Say and display the first word, for example, *said*. Ask students to say it with you. Tell students that *said* has three sounds: /s/ /ĕ/ /d/. Ask students which of the letter sounds they know and can decode (the initial /s/ and the final /d/).

4. Mark the irregular part of the word with hearts. In the word *said*, the *a* and *i* would be marked with hearts because the vowels do not follow a regular pattern and cannot be decoded. Explain that they are the tricky part that must be learned by heart.

5. Have students say the word, trace the word, and write the word on the *Heart Words Record Sheets*. Have students draw hearts over the *a* and the *i*. Then have them write *ai* in the "Tricky Part" box.

6. Repeat the process for the other Heart Words selected.

Differentiation

Heart Words will change as students learn more phonics patterns and letter-sound relationships. Elkonin Boxes (page 25) can be used for Heart Word practice. Students place the hearts in the boxes as they map the sounds and replace them with letters.

Heart Words

are	from	people	two
as	his	said	was
been	is	the	water
come	of	their	were
could	on	there	word
do	one	they	would
find	or	to	you

Name: _____ Date: _____

♡ **Heart Words Record Sheet** ♡

Directions: Listen to your teacher. Write each word. Draw hearts above tricky letters. Write the tricky letters in the boxes.

1. _____

2. _____

3. _____

4. _____

Word Show

Objectives

- Recognize and read grade-appropriate irregularly spelled words.
- Identify words with inconsistent but common spelling-sound correspondences.

Background Information

Students will analyze an irregularly spelled word, make a poster of the word, and explain unique features in the word. This in-depth look at a word and hearing what others have to say about words supports orthographic mapping, helping ensure that words are effectively stored in memory. Repeated, meaningful encounters with words in this manner develops students' sight-word banks.

Materials

- *Word Facts* (page 69)
- 9 x 12-inch construction paper
- craft supplies (crayons, markers, stickers, yarn, craft sticks, glue, tape)

Process

1. Select words students need to learn to read automatically. You may wish to use high-frequency words, words from texts students are reading, or spelling or vocabulary words. Some examples are on the chart on page 68. This activity can be done individually or in small groups.

2. Introduce the words to the students. Select one word and work together to complete a *Word Facts* activity sheet.

3. Give each student (or group) a *Word Facts* activity sheet, and assign a word to each one (or allow students to select a word from the list).

4. Have the students complete their *Word Facts* activity sheets and share what they learned.

5. Have students use the craft supplies to make posters to display their words. They should include information from the activity sheet on their posters.

6. When the posters are complete, have a "Word Show." Students take turns displaying their posters and sharing facts about their words.

7. Display the posters in the classroom. Have students practice reading the words periodically.

Differentiation

Select words students still need to learn by sight. Pair students who might need extra help with students who can work more independently. Allow more advanced readers to select their own challenging words.

Irregularly Spelled Words

a	do	of	their	water
any	does	on	there	were
are	find	one	they	what
as	from	or	to	who
been	have	people	two	words
color	his	said	very	work
come	is	some	want	would
could	many	the	was	you

Name: _____ Date: _____

Word Facts

Directions: Write your word. Answer the questions about your word.

Word:

Number of letters in the word:	Number of vowels in the word:	Number of consonants in the word:

Which letters follow a phonics rule?

Which letters do not follow a phonics rule?

Something interesting about the letters in the word:

Write a sentence with the word:

Making Phrases

Objectives

- Read with sufficient accuracy and fluency to support comprehension.
- Read grade-level text orally with accuracy, appropriate rate, and expression on successive readings.

Background Information

Reading with fluency is a foundational skill that is tied to reading success (Rasinski et al. 2017). The ability to group and read words in phrases aids in fluency, which in turn allows readers to focus on comprehension. Providing students with ways to practice automatic word recognition and appropriate phrasing is one means of building fluency. Making Phrases engages students in determining how to break sentences into phrases and practicing reading sentences with appropriate phrasing.

Most of the words in the sentences provided here come from Edward Fry's High-Frequency Instant Word List (Kress and Fry 2016). According to Fry, the first three hundred words in the list represent about 67 percent of the words students encounter when reading.

Materials

- *Let's Make Phrases* (page 72)
- markers, pens, or colored pencils of at least two colors

Process

1. Write several sentences such as these on the board or on chart paper.

    The furry dog barked at the truck.

    My little kitten hides quietly in my room.

    The blue bird sits in a nest.

    The busy children build a bridge.

    The goldfish swims in the water.

    The people march in the parade.

    My uncle plays a tuba in the band.

    The teacher likes to read funny stories.

2. Explain that when we read sentences it is important to read the words in groups rather than one by one. Model reading a sentence and pausing between the subject of the sentence and what they are doing. Read this sentence aloud as an example: *The furry dog* (pause) *barked at the truck.*

3. Read the next sentence to the class with correct phrasing. Ask students to repeat the sentence with the phrasing you used. Use your hand to chunk or scoop the phrases by making a scallop motion under groups of words.

4. Show students how to use two different colors to mark the two phrases. One phrase will include the *who* or *what* and the second phrase will tell what it is doing. Read the sentence together one more time. Repeat this process with the rest of the practice sentences.

5. Give students copies of *Let's Make Phrases*. Read the directions and monitor as students mark the phrases in each sentence. Remind them to practice reading each sentence aloud after they have marked the phrases.

6. When they finish, have students find partners and practice reading their sentences, with correct phrasing, to each other.

7. To extend and focus on comprehension, you can have students draw pictures to illustrate each sentence after they finish their fluent reading practice.

Differentiation

Slide the activity sheet into a plastic page protector for students who find making phrases difficult. Have them use erasable markers so they can easily make changes. To challenge advanced students, provide them with a copy of a poem or similar text. Ask them to mark phrases on that text and then read it aloud with appropriate phrasing.

Let's Make Phrases

Directions: Read each sentence. Draw lines under each sentence to break it into two phrases. Use two different colors for the lines.

The happy people drive to the beach.

The black cat sees the birds in the air.

The girls like to write in their notebooks.

The loud truck went down the street.

The boy read his books all day long.

The big dog ran away from the cat.

Punctuation Matters!

Objectives

- Read with sufficient accuracy and fluency to support comprehension.
- Read grade-level text orally with accuracy, appropriate rate, and expression on successive readings.

Background Information

Reading with fluency is a foundational skill that is tied to reading success (Rasinski et al. 2017). Prosody is the ability to read smoothly and with expression. Often when we read with prosody, we sound like we are having a conversation. Reading with prosody increases comprehension, as the reader is better able to make mental pictures in their mind. Providing students ways to practice prosody builds fluency. One way to do this is through repeated reading, which has been shown to increase fluency (Samuels 1979). This strategy uses familiar story sentences, allowing young readers to participate in an engaging form of repeated reading. The goal is for students to read common story sentences aloud with partners who critique their expression.

Materials

- *Story Sentence Strips* (page 75)

Process

1. Write these sample sentences on the board:

   "Who will help me cut the wheat?"
   "Quack!" squawked Mrs. Mallard, all upset. "This is no place for baby ducklings!"

2. Read the first sentence together as a group. Ask students what words and punctuation in the first sentence give clues as to how the sentence should be read. Repeat the process with the second sentence.

3. Distribute *Story Sentence Strips* to students. Have students work in pairs.

4. Students cut the sentence strips apart and place them face up in a stack.

5. Students each read the top sentence strip silently and consider how to read the sentence(s) with proper phrasing and expression.

6. Each student then reads aloud the sentence. Have students discuss how they decided to read each sentence. If there is a difference in how students read a sentence, have them discuss why.

7. Students take turns reading the rest of the sentence strips, alternating who reads aloud first.

Differentiation

Be intentional about student pairs. Stronger readers can be paired with striving readers to provide support. Some students may benefit by using sentences from stories they are familiar with. Challenge advanced readers to find their own sentences, and have them try using different punctuation when reading them aloud.

"The sky is falling! The sky is falling! We must tell the King!"

"Somebody has been eating my porridge and it's all gone!" cried Baby Bear.

"Run, run as fast as you can! You can't catch me, I'm the Gingerbread Man!"

Story Sentence Strips

Directions: Work with a partner. Cut the strips apart. Place them in a stack. Take turns drawing a strip and reading the sentences.

-- ✂ ---

Frog said, "I wrote, dear Toad, I am glad that you are my best friend. Your best friend, Frog." "Oh," said Toad, "that makes a very good letter."

- -

But the little pig says, "Not by the hair on my chinny chin chin! I will not let you in!"

- -

"This bowl of porridge is too cold! This one is too hot! But this one is just right," said Goldilocks.

- -

"The sky is falling! The sky is falling! We must tell the King!"

- -

TRIP! TRAP! TRIP! TRAP! "Who's that trip-trapping over my bridge?" shouted the troll.

- -

"I'll love you forever, I'll like you for always, as long as I'm living, my baby you'll be."

- -

"Somebody has been eating my porridge and it's all gone!" cried Baby Bear.

- -

"Run, run as fast as you can! You can't catch me, I'm the Gingerbread Man!"

- ✂ - - -

Reading Comprehension and Content Knowledge

The strategies in this section correspond with key competencies identified in *What the Science of Reading Says about Reading Comprehension and Content Knowledge* (Jump and Kopp 2023). These research-based instructional strategies will help teachers bridge the gap between the science of literacy instruction and classroom practice.

Strategy	Skills and Understandings Addressed					
	Building Content Knowledge	All About Vocabulary	Literacy Knowledge: Print Concepts to Genre Study	Language Structures: Syntax and Semantics	Text Structures and Verbal Reasoning	Reading Comprehension Strategies
Think and Draw	■					
Three Key Facts	■					
Anticipation Guide	■					
Cheat Sheet	■					
Concept of Definition Map		■				
Keywords		■				
Keyword Association		■				
Beginning and End			■			

Strategy	Skills and Understandings Addressed *(cont.)*					
	Building Content Knowledge	All About Vocabulary	Literacy Knowledge: Print Concepts to Genre Study	Language Structures: Syntax and Semantics	Text Structures and Verbal Reasoning	Reading Comprehension Strategies
Genre Basics			■			
Sentence Scramble				■		
Concept Map					■	
List-Group-Label					■	
Rank-Ordering Retell						■
Points of Confusion						■
Feature Help						■

Reading Comprehension and Content Knowledge

Simply put, reading comprehension is understanding what we read. It is the knowledge that words represent thoughts and ideas. It is the skill required for meaning-making, and meaning-making is the very heart of reading. Why read words if we cannot make meaning from them? While we may be able to define reading comprehension simply, the act is not so simple. Researchers from a variety of disciplines have attempted to describe, visualize, theorize, and model the processes that occur in a reader's mind when making meaning from words, and while there may not be a definitive model, there is much we have learned that has significant implications for instructional practices.

In order to comprehend what they read, readers must have strong foundational skills. They must have the ability to accurately and effortlessly decode most or all of the words in a text (Duke, Ward, and Pearson 2021). While decoding and fluency skills are necessary components for reading comprehension, it is widely accepted that they are not sufficient. Early readers need explicit instruction in comprehension, e.g., activating prior knowledge, summarizing, and aspects of text structure. Teachers must provide a model of thinking (metacognition) that supports students in the acquisition of the skills needed.

> Readers must be able to cognitively process the words, drawing meaning from their own experiences and knowledge to understand the author's message.

We know readers must be able to cognitively process the words, drawing meaning from their own experiences and knowledge to understand an author's message. Many agree that reading is a dialogue between the reader and the author, and during this dialogue, the reader generates questions to help anticipate meaning, search for information, respond intellectually and emotionally, and infer ideas from and explain further the content of the text. We also know that fluency can influence comprehension. A fluent reader is a reader who is understanding what they read. Understanding the words in the text—the vocabulary—impacts both fluency and comprehension.

What Is Vocabulary?

What comes to mind when you hear the word *vocabulary*? For most, the word suggests a list of words ready for use in one's speech and writing. Educators and researchers in the field of reading have long recognized that vocabulary knowledge plays an integral role in a student's ability to comprehend reading material. Students with wider vocabularies find it easier to comprehend more of what they read than do students with limited vocabularies. Moreover, students who have strong vocabularies have less difficulty learning unfamiliar words because those words are more likely to be related to words that students already know (Rupley, Logan, and Nichols 1999).

As William Nagy and Judith Scott (2000) point out, for many, the word *vocabulary* suggests a reductionist attitude toward word learning. The term *vocabulary* begs the reader to look just at words and their meanings rather than at how the words are part of the overall reading process. It also suggests that students learn words by memorizing short definitions or sentences. This limited perception about vocabulary, combined with the traditional and unsound method of introducing words and asking students to look them up in the dictionary, goes against all that is known about the reading process. The process of using word knowledge to comprehend reading is rather complex and merits discussion.

Levels of Word Knowledge

An abundance of research has demonstrated the critical role of vocabulary knowledge in reading comprehension (Cromley and Azevedo 2007; Perfetti and Stafura 2013). So much so that researchers have referred to vocabulary knowledge as the "central connection point" between a reader's word recognition knowledge and their comprehension of text (Perfetti and Stafura 2013, 24). In addition, researchers have established that there are different levels of word knowledge: unknown, acquainted, and established (Lapp, Flood, and Farnan 2008; Ryder and Graves 2003). *Unknown words* are words that students neither recognize nor understand. For instance, few kindergartners are able to define the word *symbol. Acquainted words* are those that students may recognize but must consciously think about to determine their meanings. Fourth graders are acquainted with the term *metaphor*, but they may not be able to define it in detail. *Established words* are those words that students recognize and can define easily and automatically. The word *simile* should be well established in the vocabularies of every eighth grader.

The goal is to move new vocabulary through the acquaintance level into the established level so students can use the words in their own speech and writing. To achieve this, teachers must expose students to the word a number of times and in a variety of contexts.

Knowing a word completely involves a number of skills: recognizing the word automatically; knowing the denotations, connotations, synonyms, antonyms, metaphors, and analogies for the word; associating the word with different experiences; and being able to explain one's understanding of the nuances of the word. Obviously, students cannot learn all of these skills with only a single exposure to the word (Lapp, Flood, and Farnan 2008). Word learning is an incremental process—a series of encounters that leads

> Word learning is an incremental process—a series of encounters that leads to mastery of the word.

to mastery of the word. Sometimes brief instruction just before or after reading is all that students need to develop a thorough understanding of an unknown word.

Word-Learning Tasks

In addition to different levels of word knowledge, there are different word-learning tasks that students engage in. Lapp, Flood, and Farnan (2008) categorize word learning into six distinct tasks:

- **Learning to Read Known Words**—Students may have words already in their oral vocabularies, but they may not recognize them in print. There is no need to teach the meanings of these words because students already know and understand them when they hear them; they just cannot read them. For example, students may have heard the word *ceremony* in the context of a wedding or other event, but they may not recognize it in print.

- **Learning New Meanings for Known Words**—If the new meanings of known words do not represent new and difficult concepts, teachers should acknowledge the known meaning, give the new meaning, and note the similarities between the meanings. Students usually recognize the word *practices*, and may associate it with sports teams, but they may not know it has a definition related to religion.

- **Learning New Words Representing Known Concepts**—Sometimes words are not in students' oral or reading vocabularies, but students do have prior knowledge of the concept. For example, students may not know the word *motivation*, but they know *motivate* and the suffix *–tion*, so the concept of *motivation* is present.

- **Learning New Words for New Concepts**—When students do not know the word or the concept associated with the word, they have the demanding task of learning both. For these words, it is best to build as much background knowledge as possible. For example, students probably have never heard of the word *primitive* and will need to develop the background knowledge to understand it.

- **Clarifying and Enriching the Meanings of Known Words**—As their vocabularies become more sophisticated, students begin to learn the nuances involved in words with varying shades of meaning.

- **Moving Words into Students' Expressive Vocabularies**—Beyond recognizing a word, knowing what it means, and understanding its shades of meaning is the ability to use the word in speech or in writing.

Many unknown words are academic vocabulary words. *Academic vocabulary* is specific to academic contexts and is frequently not used in normal conversation. It is important for teachers to provide direct and explicit instruction in the language of academics, especially for English learners.

Academic Vocabulary

Academic vocabulary has two components: domain-specific academic vocabulary and general academic vocabulary. Domain-specific academic vocabulary is what most of us likely consider academic vocabulary; these are low-frequency words, mostly confined to use in a specific discipline, such as math, science, or social studies (Baumann and Graves 2010). Teachers may be familiar with the terms *tier 3 words* (Beck, McKeown, and Kucan 2002) or *technical vocabulary* (Fisher and Frey 2008) to describe domain-specific academic vocabulary. Examples include words such as *acronym*, *isosceles*, or *osmosis*. This is the vocabulary one needs to learn conceptual ideas and subject-matter information.

General academic vocabulary includes words that are used across disciplines to explain and describe, and connect ideas and thoughts. These words are what many might consider markers of a sophisticated vocabulary or the language of school, sometimes referred to as *tier 2 words* (Beck, McKeown, and Kucan 2002). Examples include words such as *recognize*, *support*, and *include*. These more frequently occurring words are often parts of larger word families (*support*, *supported*, *unsupportive*), therefore, derivational and morphological knowledge are important skills for readers to acquire.

> Developing a more robust oral and written vocabulary and the skills to tackle unknown words will accelerate comprehension as students encounter increasingly complex academic and literary texts.

In the early elementary grades, vocabulary development should be considered a vital part of comprehension instruction. Suggested instruction includes (1) explicit vocabulary instruction supported with pictures and realia (real, tangible representations); (2) repeated exposures to new words; (3) multiple exposures to new words through authentic activities such as speaking, listening, and writing; and (4) the learning of strategies to understand parts of words that hold meaning (prefixes, suffixes). Developing a more robust oral and written vocabulary and the skills to tackle unknown words will accelerate comprehension as students encounter increasingly complex academic and literary texts (Kamil et al. 2008).

Comprehension Strategies

Decades of research have helped us determine what effective readers do as they read (NRP 2000). Some of the most interesting findings came from the work of Pressley and Afflerbach (1995), in which proficient readers explained what was happening in their minds while reading by thinking aloud to the researchers. From this and other studies, we have learned that good readers have prereading behaviors that include setting a purpose for reading and previewing text to take note of organizational patterns and text structure. Proficient readers draw from their prior knowledge to predict events and information, generate hypotheses as they read, and determine the meaning of unknown words or confusing phrases. They make inferences, make connections between ideas and texts, draw conclusions, and summarize. These readers ask themselves questions throughout the reading process. If we wanted to summarize these behaviors into one sentence, we would be correct in stating that *proficient readers are strategic readers.*

> Reading comprehension strategies have been defined as cognitive and metacognitive processes that readers use deliberately and consciously for the means of understanding what they are reading.

It stands to reason that teachers can develop better readers by providing strategy instruction to model and scaffold behaviors of strategic reading. Reading comprehension strategies have been defined as cognitive and metacognitive processes that readers use deliberately and consciously for the means of understanding what they are reading (Almasi and Hart 2018; Paris, Lipson, and Wixson 1983; Pressley, Borkowski, and Schneider 1987). According to Shanahan, "Strategies like monitoring, self-questioning, visualizing, comparing the text with prior knowledge, identifying text organization, and so on are all intentional, purposeful actions that are effective in improving comprehension or recall" (2018, para. 7). Teaching the following strategies to students has been shown to increase reading comprehension: activating background knowledge, making predictions, making inferences, visualizing, identifying text organization, generating questions, summarizing, and monitoring comprehension (Shanahan et al. 2010). Strategy instruction is a key part of teaching reading in the elementary grades. However, it is important to note that strategy instruction is just one component of reading comprehension instruction, and research does not recommend strategies to be taught in isolation. We teach strategies because we have learned they represent what good readers do when they read—they are strategic readers. Therefore, strategy instruction is not meant to teach readers to use a strategy but to teach them to be strategic. Almasi and Hart describe why this distinction is important: "The difference [between teaching students a 'strategy' versus teaching students to be 'strategic'] is that strategic actions require intentionality—they require a reader who is actively processing the text and making decisions about it" (2018, 228). Instruction that scaffolds students' selection of appropriate strategies, embeds strategy instruction, and involves multiple strategies is most effective.

Syntax and Semantics

An understanding of how language structure works, through the development of syntactical and semantic knowledge, aids reading comprehension. Syntax is the system of how words are arranged to make sense in a language. Syntactical knowledge includes an understanding of the functions of words and the rules of grammar that govern word arrangement, impacting and conveying meaning in a sentence. *Semantics* refers to the overall meaning of a sentence or the message the words convey. An essential part of semantic knowledge involves knowing how to determine the differences between words that convey similar meanings and understanding how these differences affect meaning, for example, knowing how the use of the word *jog* as opposed to *run* changes the meaning of the sentence. This grasp of the structure of language helps readers process and understand text at the sentence level. While vocabulary development facilitates the understanding of individual words, knowledge of language structure helps readers figure out how the arrangement of words in a sentence influences the meaning. Instructional activities that focus students' attention on the sentence level, attending to the ways words, clauses, and phrases combine to make meaning are effective in developing knowledge of language structure (LeVasseur, Macaruso, and Shankweiler 2008).

Content Knowledge

In the previous section addressing comprehension strategies, we cautioned against isolated skills instruction. If our goal is to produce competent, independent, strategic readers, then it follows that we must address the needs of the whole reader and develop their capacities to know not just *how* but *when* to use strategies. Many strategies rely on the reader activating and making connections to their background knowledge. Decades of reading research have shown us that along with decoding and fluency skills, another key to reading comprehension is the development of a broad base of knowledge readers can activate and apply to the reading situation. This knowledge includes topics such as academic vocabulary, morphology, and familiarity with text and language structures, but it also includes topical knowledge. Wattenberg points out that "as students age and gain basic skills, the lack of knowledge typically becomes the much greater obstacle to good reading" (2016, 2).

> When students have knowledge of facts, ideas, and concepts across content areas, they can develop an understanding of how concepts/topics are related, how they are explained, how processes work, and more.

Current state standards have shifted the focus at the elementary grades from fiction to informational text. A broad base of content or topical knowledge can give readers a comprehension advantage when they encounter a diversity of topics, particularly in science and social studies. Research demonstrates that having schema (relevant prior knowledge) for a topic aids not only in the comprehension process but also in the learning process (Anderson and Nagy 1992; Anderson and Pearson 1984; Kintsch 1988). When a topic or concept is introduced in text and students can initiate the retrieval process (activating their schema for the topic), they have an anchor to which they can connect the new information to better understand it (Anderson and Pearson 1984). Think of our schema as a set of folders in a filing cabinet (or in our "cloud storage"): it is easier for us to add items to our existing folders than it is to create a new folder with a new label and find things to fill it with. This is an overly simplistic but helpful analogy for thinking about the importance of schema. The advantage this broad knowledge bestows goes beyond the facts and information of a topic. When students have knowledge of facts, ideas, and concepts across content areas, they can develop an understanding of how concepts/topics are related, how they are explained, how processes work, and more. This familiarity can be transferred to new topics and content to facilitate learning.

Content and concept knowledge can support incidental word learning. When students have knowledge of a concept or topic, that information allows them to better understand new vocabulary or technical vocabulary related to that concept. This knowledge of related words can activate broader semantic networks (the organization of facts and knowledge in the mind) to enhance comprehension and accelerate new learning (Cervetti, Wright, and Hwang 2016; Willingham 2006). Concept and content knowledge will also assist readers in understanding words with multiple meanings. For example, exposure to and broad knowledge of marine life can help a reader distinguish the differing meanings of the word *school*, as in a *school of fish* as opposed to an *elementary school*. Similarly, familiarity with a topic can help students understand figurative language, distinguish that a statement is indeed figurative and not literal, and interpret the meaning of the figurative statement. For example, students read that a team of scientists really "hit it out of the park" with the results of their latest study. Exposure to or familiarity with baseball would help these students understand (1) that this is a figurative statement—that the scientists did not actually hit anything, and an actual park was not involved—and (2) that their results were significant and considered remarkable.

The recommendations for supporting content learning are related to those for teaching reading comprehension. It is not possible that we could teach students all of the facts, information, and concepts they are likely to encounter in every piece of text! Therefore, isolated instruction is not beneficial. Embedded strategy instruction is the key. Embedding this instruction in a wide variety of text genres and providing exposure to multiple texts develops layers and depth of knowledge. The recognition of the importance of building a broad base of content knowledge is part of the push for an increase in the amount of informational text students engage with during elementary school. Informational text also allows for instruction in different genres and text structures, furthering students' knowledge of organizational patterns, language structures, and knowledge across domains.

The strategies in this chapter are intended to develop competent, independent, strategic readers who can understand and learn from a diversity of texts across a wide variety of topics. This type of reader can flexibly and independently employ various strategies when reading, making decisions about which strategies to use and switching between strategies when necessary. Great teachers know that some strategies work for some students and other strategies work for other students, just as some strategies work best with certain types of reading material. The most important thing to remember when trying to improve reading comprehension in students is that the skill level, group dynamic, and makeup of students should determine the approach to take and which modifications to lessons may be needed.

> The recognition of the importance of building a broad base of content knowledge is part of the push for an increase in the amount of informational text students engage with during elementary school.

Think and Draw

Objectives

- Identify the main topic and retell key details of a text.
- Identify the main purpose of a text, including what the author wants to answer, explain, or describe.

Background Information

Thinking and drawing about a text are strategies that build knowledge and understanding of what is being read (McConnell 1993; Stahl 2014). Prior to reading, the teacher leads a discussion and has students draw pictures of their background knowledge (schema), helping them make connections between what they know and what they will read. During and after reading, students draw what they learn and compare and contrast their initial ideas and questions with the new information. This technique helps new information remain in long-term memory because students have made the connections. All students, but particularly emergent learners, benefit from being provided with another way to express their ideas. Think and Draw walks students through these steps as they closely read a teacher-selected text.

Materials

- *Think and Draw* (page 89)
- sticky notes
- two text selections

Process

1. Select two texts—nonfiction works best for this lesson—and give each student a copy of the first. Display the *Think and Draw* activity sheet.

2. Ask students to look at the text and identify the topic. Complete the topic section of the displayed activity sheet.

3. Tell students to close their eyes and allow their minds to make mental pictures of the topic. Have them share their ideas and ask one or two students to draw pictures in the "Before Reading: What I know" section. Repeat this process to complete "Before Reading: What I think and wonder." Guide students to give ideas or make predictions about what they might learn from reading this text.

4. Give each student three or four sticky notes. Direct students to read the text. As students read, have them draw pictures of facts or ideas they find on the sticky notes. Allow them to share these with partners, and then add them to the "During Reading" section of the displayed activity sheet.

5. Have students finish reading the text. Ask them to share what they learned, and have a few students write their responses in "After Reading: What I learned."

6. After completing the process as a whole group, give students their own copies of the *Think and Draw* activity sheet. Have students read a different text selection and complete their activity sheets. When finished, have partners share their thoughts and learnings.

Differentiation

Carefully select the texts you use for this activity. You may need to introduce key vocabulary to students who are learning English. Rather than having students work independently, you could have them work with partners or small groups. You may want to let most of the class work on their own while doing the group lesson with students who need additional support. Allow students who do not like drawing to sketch simple pictures and add details with text.

Think and Draw Example

Topic: What I will read about _____ butterflies _____

Before Reading: What I know

Before Reading: What I think and wonder

Where do they live?

How do they grow?

What do they eat?

During Reading: Facts or ideas from the text

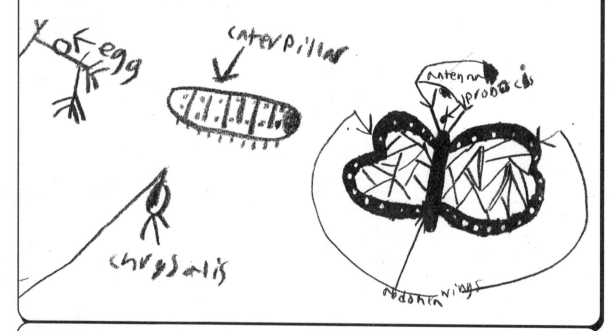

After Reading: What I learned

A butterfly starts as an egg. The egg hatches into a caterpillar.
The caterpillar eats and grows. Then it becomes a chrysalis.
After staying inside for about two weeks, a butterfly comes out.
The butterfly has wings, an abdomen, and antennae. A butterfly
eats with a proboscis.

Name: _____ Date: _____

Think and Draw

Directions: Draw and write about the text.

Topic: What I will read about _____

Before Reading: What I know	**Before Reading:** What I think and wonder

During Reading: Facts or ideas from the text

After Reading: What I learned

Three Key Facts

Objectives

- Recount or describe key ideas or details from a text read aloud or information presented orally or through another media.

- Ask and answer questions about what a speaker says in order to clarify comprehension, gather additional information, or deepen understanding of a topic or issue.

- Integrate and evaluate content presented in diverse media and formats, including visually and quantitatively as well as in words.

Background Information

Three Key Facts builds background knowledge by using multimedia resources. Background knowledge plays a vital role in reading comprehension, listening comprehension, and continued learning of more complex concepts and ideas. In addition to detailed concept knowledge, students need broad knowledge of a variety of topics, ideas, and concepts to allow them to read material aimed at a "general audience" (Hirsch 2006). Creators of content rely on the notion that their readers or viewers bring with them some relevant background knowledge they can apply to understand the material. Yet teachers cannot teach every conceivable topic students need to have a broad base of background knowledge. This strategy helps students gain broad understanding of topics by viewing informational videos and focusing on key facts.

Materials

- short informational video
- Three Key Facts activity sheet (created by teacher), optional

Process

1. Select a video clip on a relevant topic. Ideally, the clip will be more than two minutes but less than five minutes and will have specific facts for students to identify. Short videos help students more easily identify key information.

2. Develop a prompt that focuses students on the type of information they need to find. For example, if students are watching a short video related to communities and transportation, you might prompt them to identify three forms of transportation.

   Example: *As you watch this short video about communities and transportation, find three ways you can get from here to there (three forms of transportation).*

3. Provide students with the prompt, either written on the board or on a teacher-made activity sheet. Explain that they are going to watch the video, listen for three key facts, and record the facts. Tell students that these three facts are "key takeaways." They are broad, major ideas related to a topic rather than discrete details or facts.

4. Show the video, and have students record their facts. When finished, have students share with partners or small groups. Then, discuss the key facts as a whole class.

5. Provide students the opportunity to use this background knowledge multiple times through reading relevant texts, in their writing, or by engaging in extended learning on a related topic.

Differentiation

Provide background knowledge to students who may have limited knowledge of the subject. Scaffold the process as needed by providing sentence stems or suggested vocabulary to accompany the activity sheet. When watching the video, pause at select points, and have students partner with one another to identify and discuss important information. Challenge advanced students to provide details for one of the facts.

Anticipation Guide

Objectives

- Identify the main topic of a text. Ask and answer such questions as *who, what, where, when, why,* and *how* to demonstrate understanding of key details in a text.
- Describe the connection between events, concepts, or steps in a process in a text.
- Integrate and evaluate content presented in diverse media and formats, including visually and quantitatively as well as in words.

Background Information

Anticipation Guides increase interest, develop motivation, and engage students. They encourage students to express opinions, make connections to prior knowledge, and make predictions about the topic they will study. This variation incorporates multimedia resources such as websites and video or audio clips and focuses students on engaging with the content rather than being passive observers. Using multimedia resources supports the building of background knowledge by both activating knowledge students may have and frontloading information for students with limited or surface knowledge of a topic. Students first take a position on several statements. They engage with multimedia and then respond to the statements again, using their new knowledge to support their responses. Anticipation Guides help set a purpose for engaging with multimedia as students view or listen to find information that supports or challenges their positions.

Materials

- multimedia source (video, audio clip, website to explore)
- Anticipation Guide (created by teacher)

Process

1. Identify a multimedia resource related to the topic of study and preview it to determine important concepts students should focus on. Prepare an Anticipation Guide of several short statements about these concepts or ideas. (See examples on pages 93–94.) The statements should be designed to activate prior knowledge students may have about the topic. True/false or agree/disagree statements work best. Present the statements in the order in which the ideas appear in the resource.

2. Distribute Anticipation Guides to students. Working with the whole class, teach students to use the Anticipation Guide. Read the statements aloud and have students respond in the "Before" column. Ask students to share their responses in a class discussion.

3. Have students engage with the multimedia selection as a class, individually, or with partners as appropriate. Tell students they should look or listen for evidence that supports or refutes their "Before" responses. Have students complete the "After" column on the guide as they discover evidence.

4. Engage in a collaborative discussion about the "After" answers, asking students to explain their thinking. Ask students if they changed their responses as a result of the multimedia resource, and if so, why.

Differentiation

- With new or particularly challenging topics, you may wish to scaffold learning by preparing stopping points in the multimedia resource, guiding students step by step through the content in smaller chunks. Alternately, students can work in groups to respond to the Anticipation Guide after they engage with the resource.

- As an extension, have students write about whether their new learning supports their "Before" opinions, citing evidence from the resource. Students should be allowed to disagree with information they heard if they can successfully create an argument and support it with details.

Examples

True/False Anticipation Guide

Before		Statement	After	
True	False		True	False
		It is helpful for children my age to set goals. How I know		
		It is easy to tell how someone feels by looking at them. How I know:		
		I know ways to solve problems with friends. How I know:		

Agree/Disagree Anticipation Guide

Before		Statement	After	
Agree	Disagree		Agree	Disagree
		It is important to ride a bike that is the right size for you. How I know:		
		If you are a good bike rider, you don't need your helmet. How I know:		
		Kids also need to wear helmets when they ride their scooters or skate. How I know:		
		It doesn't matter where you ride your bike. How I know:		

Cheat Sheet

Objectives

- Identify the main topic of a text. Ask and answer such questions as *who, what, where, when, why,* and *how* to demonstrate understanding of key details in a text.

- Integrate and evaluate content presented in diverse media and formats, including visually and quantitatively as well as in words.

Background Information

Cheat Sheet is a strategy to support students in building knowledge of a topic before, during, and after reading. Prior knowledge of a topic is a critical factor in reading comprehension (Wexler 2019). Many strategies rely on activating prior knowledge, but sometimes students come to a topic with very limited background. Research demonstrates that teaching words in categories, engaging students in topic-focused wide reading, and incorporating multimedia are effective strategies for building knowledge (Neuman, Kaefer, and Pinkham 2014). Cheat Sheet includes and builds on all three of these practices. This strategy can be used over several lessons or an entire unit, and it can be used to support a particularly complex text.

Materials

- Cheat Sheet activity sheet (created by teacher)
- multimedia resources for students to explore

Process

1. Create a Cheat Sheet to introduce a topic (see example on page 97). The Cheat Sheet can include background information, links to multimedia resources, between three to five key vocabulary words, questions to focus attention on important ideas, and sentence frames.

2. Working with the whole class, teach students to use the Cheat Sheet. Give each student a copy. Introduce the topic with a brief explanation and review the information. Pronounce each vocabulary word for students, and review the sheet together before engaging in content learning activities.

3. As a group, preview the resources in the General Background section. Encourage students to use the back of the sheet to take notes as they read and view the background materials.

4. After engaging with the resources, discuss what students learned and help them define vocabulary words and answer the questions. Work together to write a sentence summarizing the topic.

5. During a future lesson, students can complete a Cheat Sheet in small groups or on their own. Give students time to review the background information, take notes, define the key terms, and answer the questions.

6. When students have completed their activity, bring the group together to discuss what was learned and write summary sentences. Explain to students they will continue to use the Cheat Sheet to record ideas and details as they learn them throughout the study of the topic.

Differentiation

- Provide additional support during small-group instruction by explaining challenging topics, defining vocabulary, and using sentence stems. It may also be beneficial for some students to work on the Cheat Sheet with partners.

- As students become more skilled in using Cheat Sheets as a knowledge-building strategy, you may wish to have students write some of their own questions, use the stems as starters for small-group discussions, expand their summaries, or find additional resources to share with their classmates.

- Provide the Cheat Sheet in a digital format, giving students easier access to digital content to support the building of background knowledge and learning connections.

Cheat Sheet Example

Topic: American Symbols: The Bald Eagle

General Background

Look at the <u>map</u> to see where bald eagles live.

Check out this <u>information</u> about bald eagles.

Watch this <u>video</u>.

Define the keywords.

Things to Consider

- What important information are you learning? What questions do you have?

- What connections are you making to what you already know?

Bald Eagles	Keywords
Bald eagles are a national symbol of the United States. They are birds of prey. They mate for life and return to their same large nest. They live for 30 years and make their nest larger each year. Bald eagles were in danger of going extinct but were protected and are now no longer endangered.	bird of prey— warm-blooded— carnivore— extinct—

Questions

1. List some characteristics of bald eagles.

_____

2. Where are bald eagles found?

_____

3. What do bald eagles eat?

_____

4. Why did bald eagles almost go extinct? What changed for them?

_____

Concept of Definition Map

Objectives

- With support from adults, demonstrate understanding of word relationships and nuances in word meanings.

Background Information

The Concept of Definition Map (Nagy and Scott 2000; Schwartz and Raphael 1985) is a graphic organizer used to teach the definitions of essential academic vocabulary terms. The map is a scaffold to move the responsibility for determining the meaning of important words from the teacher to the students. In addition, students learn the subtleties and nuances of particular words, which are reinforced by the visual presentation of the information in a graphic organizer. Students learn to sort words into categories, define them by key attributes, and identify real-life connections between the words and their uses. The analogies that students create promote long-term memory by personalizing the association of the concept.

Materials

- *Concept of Definition Map* (page 100)

Process

1. Choose a concept word that will be used with the map. Write it on the board. Distribute the *Concept of Definition Map* to students. Have students write the concept word in the box at the top of the map.

2. Discuss the first question: "What is it?" Have students share what they think with partners. Elicit answers from partners for the whole class to hear. Assist students in crafting a short sentence that defines what the concept is, and have them write it on the map.

3. Repeat the process for the question "What is it like?"

4. Ask, "What are some examples?" and have students write or illustrate their responses.

5. Once students have practiced this mapping process several times, they can complete Concept of Definition Maps with partners, without teacher support.

Differentiation

Support students by providing images or videos of the concept word. Some students may benefit from sentence frames and a word bank. Advanced students can complete the map independently.

Concept of Definition Map *Example*

Word: rural

What is it?

A rural area is away from the cities where houses are more spread out.

What is it like?

Rural areas are like the country.

What are some examples?

Farms and small towns are rural.

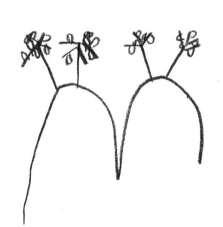

Name: _____ Date: _____

Concept of Definition Map

Directions: Write the word. Answer the questions. Draw examples of the word.

Word:

What is it?	**What is it like?**

What are some examples?

Keywords

Objectives

- Determine the meaning of words and phrases in a text relevant to a grade-level topic or subject area.

Background Information

The Keywords strategy (Hoyt 2002) helps students conduct a close read of a text and generate a list of keywords from it. From the list, they identify one academic vocabulary word that is most important. Students then use the list to create a written or oral summary. The strategy is effective because it helps students locate the most important concepts (academic vocabulary), encourages them to use their own words to summarize, and engages them in spending time reading and processing information in texts.

Materials

- text selection that is grade-level appropriate
- *Finding Keywords* (page 103)

Process

1. Provide students with a text to read. As a group, read the text closely (read-aloud or choral reading). Have students find important words in the text.

2. Ask students to share the words they selected with the group. List the words on the board. Discuss the value of each word, and ask students to explain and justify their choices to the class. As a group, determine the four most important words. Circle these.

3. Together, review the four words and identify one keyword that best summarizes the text.

4. Demonstrate how to write a summary based on the three words and the keyword. Show students how to combine information and use their own words to write the summary.

5. After students have practiced this process with the whole class, they can work independently to read a text selection and complete the *Finding Keywords* activity sheet.

Differentiation

If students are able to complete the task independently, allow them to do so while you are demonstrating the lesson to those who need support. Carefully select the text to ensure it matches students' reading abilities. If students are reading nonfiction and struggling to find keywords, tell them to look for words that are bold or italic.

Finding Keywords Example

Important Words:

seeds	blow
plants	carry
travel	float

Keyword: seeds

My Summary:

Plant seeds travel to find new places to grow. Some seeds travel by blowing in the air, but other seeds are carried by animals. Some seeds float on water.

My Picture:

Name: _____ Date: _____

Finding Keywords

Directions: List important words from the text. Choose one keyword that is most important. Use the words to write a summary. Draw a picture to match.

Important Words:

_____   _____

_____   _____

My Keyword: _____

My Summary:

_____

_____

_____

My Picture:

Keyword Association

Objectives

- Determine or clarify the meaning of words and phrases, choosing flexibly from an array of strategies, including the use of glossaries and beginning dictionaries.

Background Information

To foster robust vocabulary learning in classrooms, it is essential to build "word consciousness" in students. As Graves and Watts-Taffe (2008) shared, word consciousness is an awareness of and interest in words around you. To this end, the Keyword Association strategy facilitates content-area vocabulary recognition, recall, and comprehension by enabling students to make mental connections between unfamiliar words and familiar words. To strengthen the relationship between the two words, students create mental images or sentences combining them.

Materials

- content-area text
- *Linking Keywords* (page 107)

Process

1. Model the strategy with the whole class before having students use it on their own.

2. After reading a content-area text, have students identify unknown words from the passage. Encourage students to select words that play an important role in the text. You want them to find words with meanings that will facilitate their overall comprehension rather than arbitrary or insignificant words. List their words on the board.

3. Draw on the board three boxes with arrows between them (see page 107).

4. Write and define one of the unknown words in the first box. You may choose to define words through a collaborative class discussion or by having students use a dictionary.

5. Think of and write a keyword associated with the new word in the second box.

6. In the last box, illustrate or write a sentence to show the relationship between the two words.

7. Distribute copies of *Linking Keywords* to students. Have them select an unknown word from the list on the board, define the word they selected, and then write a word that is related to it. Finally, students draw a picture or write a sentence to show the relationship between the words.

Differentiation

Prior to the lesson, discuss the topic and activate prior knowledge with students who are learning English. Preteach dictionary-use skills to advanced students. These students can be paired with other students to help teach them dictionary use. Guide the selection of unknown words to be sure students are working with words that match their learning levels. Some students will benefit from working with partners to complete *Linking Keywords*.

Linking Keywords Example

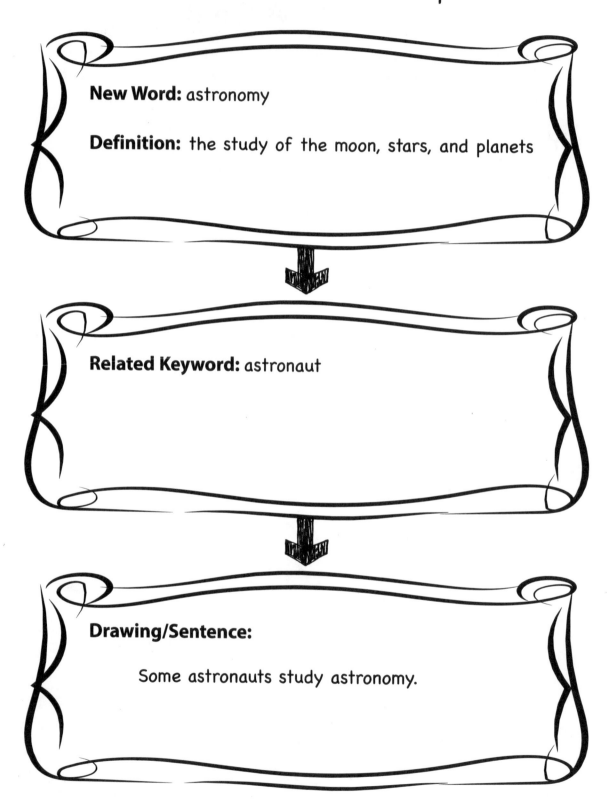

New Word: astronomy

Definition: the study of the moon, stars, and planets

Related Keyword: astronaut

Drawing/Sentence:

Some astronauts study astronomy.

Name: _____ Date: _____

Linking Keywords

Directions: Write the word and its definition. Write a related word.
Draw a picture or write a sentence that combines the words.

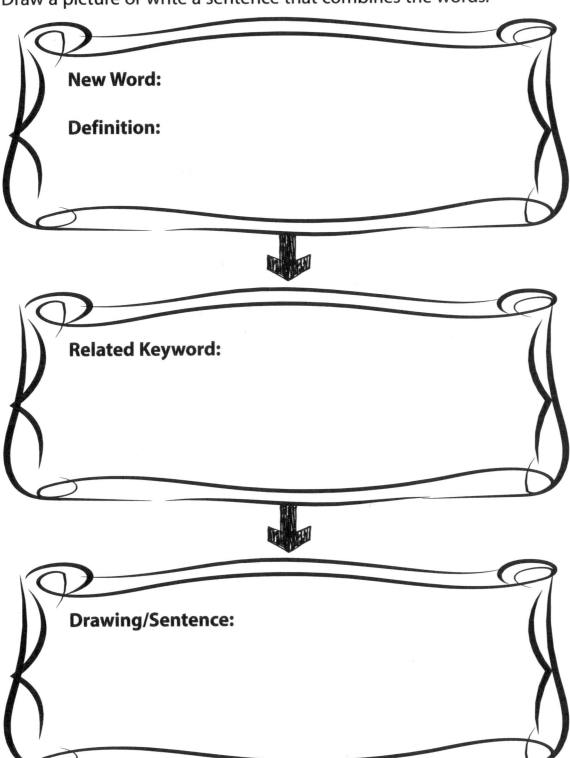

New Word:

Definition:

Related Keyword:

Drawing/Sentence:

Beginning and End

Objectives

- Know and use various text features to locate key facts or information in a text.

- Use glossaries and beginning dictionaries to determine or clarify the meaning of words and phrases.

Background Information

As students navigate informational texts, they will often encounter features and components that help them better understand the content. Students need knowledge and skills in using these text features to support reading comprehension (Kelley and Clausen-Grace 2008). The Beginning and End strategy engages students in using a text feature at the beginning of a book (table of contents) and a text feature at the end of the book (glossary) to aid in comprehension.

Materials

- nonfiction texts with a table of contents and glossary
- *At the Beginning* (page 110)
- *At the End* (page 111)

Process

1. Show students a nonfiction book and explain that it contains many features that can help them understand its contents better. Tell students that this strategy focuses on the table of contents, a text feature at the beginning of a book, and the glossary, a text feature at the end of a book.

2. Display an enlarged copy of a table of contents. Explain that the table of contents can help students get an idea of what they will learn when they read. It also helps readers know how to find information in a text.

3. Have students take turns reading the chapter titles in the table of contents. Lead a discussion about what students already know related to the contents and what they think they might learn in each chapter.

4. Challenge students to find specific information in the table of contents by asking questions about where to find things. Here are some question starters:

   - What is the topic of chapter ___?
   - Where can you learn about ___?
   - If you want to find information about ___, where would you look?

5. Display an enlarged glossary page. Tell students that the glossary is at the end of the book and that it explains what words mean. Select a word in the glossary. Have one student read aloud the word and the definition. As a whole class, talk about the word and practice using it in a sentence. Tell students they can check the glossary to learn the meanings of words.

6. Provide students with copies of *At the Beginning* and books with tables of contents and glossaries. Have students create and answer questions about the table of contents.

7. Distribute copies of *At the End*. Have students find words in the glossary and complete the page.

8. After students have completed the two activity sheets, lead a class discussion. Ask students to share what they have learned about the text features and tell the class how they will use the features when reading.

Differentiation

Carefully select the books you give to students who are learning English or are striving readers. You may want to allow these students to work with partners. Provide question starters to students for the *At the Beginning* activity sheet and preselect words for the *At the End* activity sheet. After advanced students have asked and answered questions about the table of contents, challenge them to use their answers to find information in the text.

Name: _____ Date: _____

At the Beginning

Directions: Read the Table of Contents. Write questions about it. Ask a classmate to read the Table of Contents and answer your questions.

Book Title: _____

Question	Answer
1.	
2.	
3.	
4.	

At the End

Directions: Select three words from the glossary. Write each word and its meaning. Write a sentence using each word. Draw a matching picture. Explain your words to a partner.

Word	**Picture**
Meaning	
Sentence	

Word	**Picture**
Meaning	
Sentence	

Word	**Picture**
Meaning	
Sentence	

Genre Basics

Objectives

- Read and comprehend literature.
- Explain major differences between genres, drawing on a wide reading of a range of text types.

Background Information

Early on, students are taught the differences between fiction and nonfiction. As they grow as readers, they also need to learn about the different genres of fiction and nonfiction. Knowing the features of different genres and understanding how they function aids students in comprehending what they read (Dewitz et al. 2020; Shanahan et al. 2010). Students who understand different genres will know how to approach each as they read and apply appropriate strategies to help understand the text. The Genre Basics strategy helps students focus on features of several fiction genres and learn how to apply this knowledge to their reading. Use this strategy after students have had instruction and experiences with a range of fiction and nonfiction texts.

Materials

- an assortment of fiction texts of different genres (realistic, fable/folktale, fantasy, mystery, graphic novel)
- *Fiction Favorite* (page 114)

Process

1. Briefly review the characteristics of fiction and nonfiction. Ask students to name their favorite fiction books and share how they know the books are fiction. Tell students that during this activity they are going to explore different types of fiction.

2. Write the headings *realistic, fable/folktale, fantasy, mystery,* and *graphic novel* on a chart. Discuss each genre with students.

   - realistic fiction: events could happen; characters act like real people
   - fable/folktale: teaches a lesson; explains how something came to be; characters are often animals
   - fantasy: not realistic; may have talking animals, magic, or an enchanted world
   - mystery: has a puzzling event, a case to be solved, or clues to piece together
   - graphic novel: many images on each page; speech and thought bubbles; word art

3. Assign students to small groups. Distribute a few different types of fiction texts to each group. Ask students to work with their groups to identify the types of fiction and determine features of each.

4. Have groups tell the class about the books they examined. List the books and features under the corresponding headings on the chart. Lead a class conversation on how knowledge of the characteristics can help them in their reading.

5. Have students choose a text they have read and complete *Fiction Favorite* to describe it. In the following weeks as students select fiction texts to read, encourage them to identify the types of fiction and state what features they expect to find in the texts.

Differentiation

Provide striving readers with books they are familiar with to analyze. Encourage advanced students to find and read other types of fiction.

Name: _____ Date: _____

Fiction Favorite

Directions: Read a story. Choose a word from the word bank to tell what kind of story it is. Write about the story.

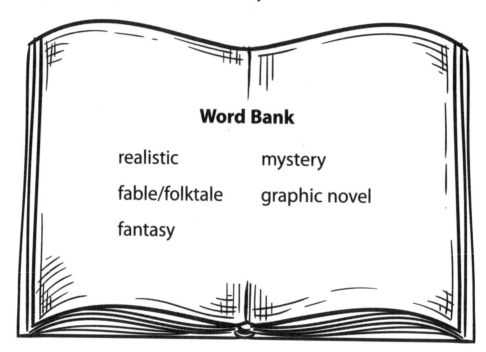

Word Bank

realistic   mystery

fable/folktale   graphic novel

fantasy

Title: _____

Type of Story: _____

How I Know the Type of Story: _____

_____

_____

_____

_____

Literacy Strategies—131697

Sentence Scramble

Objectives

- Demonstrate command of the conventions of standard English grammar and usage when writing or speaking.
- Demonstrate understanding of word relationships and nuances in word meanings.

Background Information

Knowledge of sentence structure—how words and phrases are combined to make meaning—contributes to effective word reading and reading comprehension (Moats 2020; Scarborough 2001). With Sentence Scramble, the teacher selects a sentence, scrambles the words, and has students place them in order to make meaningful sentences. Choose sentences from familiar texts used for reading or read-alouds or write them using words encountered in recent word study or vocabulary lessons.

Materials

- sentence strips

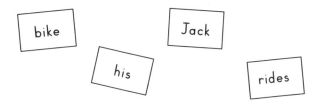

Process

1. Prepare by writing or finding sentences that incorporate words students are learning. Begin with short sentences of four or five words.

2. Display the words for one sentence out of order.

3. Ask students to unscramble the words to make a sentence that makes sense. Write the unscrambled sentence on the board, and read it aloud together.

4. Ask students *who*, *what*, *where*, *why*, and *when* questions about the sentence to help build their awareness of the different sentence parts.

5. Repeat the process for the other sentences. Gradually increase the number of words in the sentences. This strategy can also be used with sentences or vocabulary from social studies and science texts.

Differentiation

For students who need additional support, it may be helpful to write the sentences on sentence strips, cut them apart, and have students rearrange them to find the correct order. Include capital letters and punctuation as clues to the word order. Words can also be color coded by parts of speech. Challenge advanced students by asking them to select sentences from books they are reading, scramble the words, and then give them to partners to unscramble.

Concept Map

Objectives

- Identify the main topic of a text as well as key details and the focus of specific paragraphs within the text.

- Use details in a story to describe its characters, setting, or events.

Background Information

Concept Maps are effective for visually organizing information related to concepts discussed in informational texts (Hattie 2009; Horton et al. 1993). Concept Maps can be used to generate discussion around a topic prior to reading and to build students' conceptual knowledge, which better prepares students to understand what they are reading. As students read from a text, they identify relationships or links among the new concepts they learn. Concept Maps also help students develop organizational skills because they can view the concepts and details in terms of how they relate to one another in a visual format.

Materials

- chart paper and markers
- text selection

Process

1. Review the material students will be reading. Identify the important concepts in the reading, and note the ideas, words, and phrases that are related to these concepts.

2. Explain the purpose of a Concept Map to students, and discuss how it can be used as a learning tool. Present the topic of the Concept Map and discuss its relationship to the text students will be reading. Ask students to share their prior knowledge and ideas related to the topic. Create a partial Concept Map on chart paper, incorporating students' ideas.

3. Have students read the text you've selected.

4. After reading, have students share new information they learned. Add this new learning to the class map. Working together, identify the relationships and connections between concepts. Ask questions such as the following:

   - Why does this information belong on the map? How do you know?

   - Where could we place ____? Why does it belong there?

5. Distribute paper and provide students time to recreate the Concept Map. Give students time to review the Concept Map and discuss with partners, encouraging them to explain their understandings of the topic in their own words.

Differentiation

It may be useful to preview some of the information with students who need extra support. Discuss specific concepts and connections with these students before engaging in the whole-class discussion. Challenge advanced students to color code the relationships represented on the map.

Concept Map Example

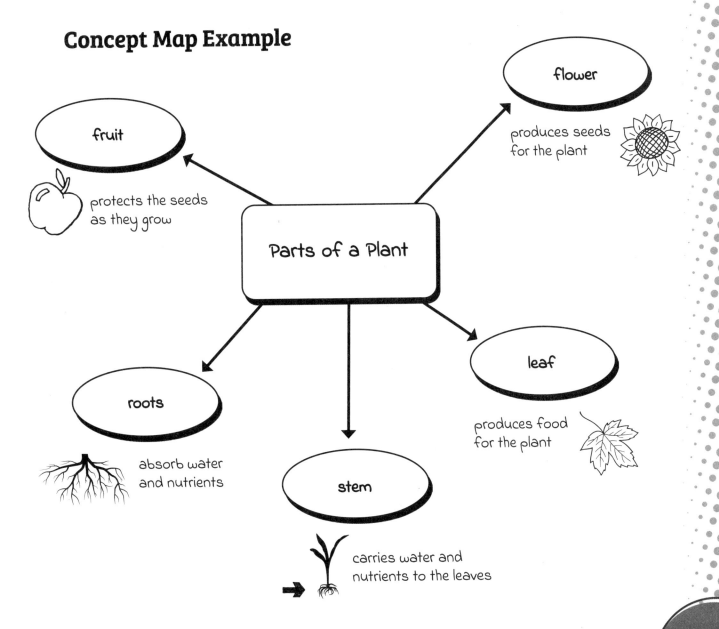

List-Group-Label

Objectives

- Sort words into categories, define words by category and one or more key attributes, and identify real-life connections between words and their use.

Background Information

List-Group-Label can be used to bridge content areas and to assess and build on prior knowledge. It combines brainstorming and classification to help students organize related concepts and to integrate and evaluate content presented in different formats, including lists. Allowing students to determine the classifications aids them in organizing and understanding information they have read (Fisher and Frey 2020; Nesbit and Adesope 2006). List-Group-Label works best when students have some background knowledge related to the concepts, but it can also be used to introduce or review concepts. Students think about hierarchical relationships among concept words and place the terms into various categories.

Materials

- science or social studies text
- *List-Group-Label Record Sheet* (page 120)

Process

1. Have students read the text. Then, distribute the *List-Group-Label Record Sheet*.

2. Provide a word or phrase from the text that describes the topic, and have students write it on their record sheets. Work with students to generate words or phrases they associate with the topic. Have students record each word or phrase in the list section. Encourage students to generate fifteen to twenty words or phrases.

3. Have students evaluate the items in the list and determine categories by considering the attributes, characteristics, and features they have in common. Have students write the categories on the record sheet and list the words in their corresponding categories. Students may generate additional words for the categories and reorganize the categories and words by combining or deleting categories.

Differentiation

Meet with students who need additional support in a small group. Have them write the words on index cards and work together to categorize them. Encourage advanced students to reclassify the words into alternate categories.

List-Group-Label Record Sheet *Example*

Topic: Animals

List of Words

giraffes	penguins	lions	chickens
parrots	coyotes	dolphins	monkeys
dogs	lizards	sharks	geese
alligators	fish	peacocks	

Group

giraffes

lions

coyotes

monkeys

dogs

Label

fur

Group

dolphins

lizards

sharks

alligators

fish

Label

scales/skin

Group

penguins

chickens

parrots

geese

peacocks

Label

feathers

List-Group-Label Record Sheet

Directions: Write the topic. List words about the topic. Group the words into categories. Label each group.

Topic: _____

List of Words

Group	Group	Group

Label	Label	Label

Rank-Ordering Retell

Objectives

- Identify the main topic of a text as well as key details and the focus of specific paragraphs within the text.

Background Information

Students need to learn to evaluate how important the ideas in the text are to effectively summarize what they have read. Rank-Ordering Retell (Hoyt 2002) assists students in learning to identify the main idea and supporting details. Students write phrases they consider to be important to the topic and then categorize the phrases as most important, moderately important, or least important. Key details, central messages, and lessons from the text should always be classified as most important, while less important details and nonessential information should be placed in the moderately important or least important categories. Rank-Ordering Retell is a flexible strategy that can be used with literary and informational texts.

Materials

- 2 x 6-inch strips of paper; six for each student
- text selection
- *Rank-Ordering Retell* (page 124)

Process

1. Complete this activity as a whole class several times before releasing it to students to work in pairs.

2. Distribute six strips of paper to each student.

3. Have students read a text. Ask them to write phrases they consider important to the topic on the strips of paper. The phrases can be taken directly from the reading or inferred by students.

4. Provide students the *Rank-Ordering Retell* activity sheet. Have students review, evaluate, and sort the phrases they wrote into three categories: most important, moderately important, and least important. Instruct them to identify the most important and least important first, as this is the easiest way to evaluate the information.

5. Have students justify their decision to put the phrases in the different categories. Discuss with students which ideas would be the most helpful if they had to write summaries.

Differentiation

Scaffold the task for students who need support by helping them identify some of the important ideas. Challenge advanced students to write summaries based on how they categorized the phrases.

Rank-Ordering Retell *Example*

Most Important Ideas

Animals need shelter to be safe.

Moderately Important Ideas

Plants are shelters.

Least Important Ideas

Animals use plants like trees to be safe. Animals use plants and logs for their homes.

Name: _____ Date: _____

Rank-Ordering Retell

Directions: Read the text. Write important ideas from the text on strips of paper. Sort the ideas into the groups below.

Most Important Ideas

Moderately Important Ideas

Least Important Ideas

Points of Confusion

Objectives

- Determine the meaning of words or phrases in a text relevant to a grade-level topic or subject area.

Background Information

Teachers must create learning environments where students feel safe and valued. Tapping the social-emotional side of learning can build relationships and create a classroom setting that encourages students to take risks (Doyle and Bramwell 2006). The Points of Confusion strategy seeks to address this by providing students with a way to identify and clarify confusing words and concepts. Students first scan a new text selection, looking for words or phrases that they think might be unclear to someone else. Then, the class works together to clarify the puzzling words or concepts, thereby activating prior knowledge through a collective experience. At the end, students record their new knowledge about words or concepts. This strategy helps students identify areas of confusion in a safe manner, activate their prior knowledge, and learn the meaning of unknown words and concepts prior to reading.

Materials

- text selection
- *Points of Confusion* (page 127)

Process

1. Draw the Points of Confusion chart (page 126) on the board. Provide students with the text they will read. Explain that when readers *preview* a text, they look at it to find words they may not know. Let students know that when they preview, they do not need to read to understand but rather pick out words that may be challenging.

2. Think aloud as you model previewing the first section of the text looking for words or concepts that might be unknown. List the words on the chart.

3. Distribute copies of *Points of Confusion* to students. Have students preview the rest of the text, looking for keywords or concepts that might be confusing to them or their classmates. Tell students to record these on their *Points of Confusion* activity sheets.

4. When students finish reading, have them share their ideas while you record them on the displayed chart.

5. Ask students to add concepts from the class chart to their own charts. Discuss each topic. During the discussion, students should write about the meaning of each word or phrase in the "Notes about the Meaning" column.

6. Determine how the text will be read—as a whole group, in pairs, or independently—and allow time for students to read the text. Remind students to refer to their charts to help them gain additional clarity on the points of confusion.

7. After reading, discuss information students found in the text that helped them better understand the points of confusion.

Differentiation

Support students by meeting in a small group to preview the text together and build background knowledge. Allow readers who need additional help to work with partners or in a small group with you to find confusing words. Write notes in the "Notes about the Meaning" column for students to record if needed.

Example

Confusing Words and Ideas	Notes about the Meaning
germination	to begin to grow
sprout	a plant coming out of the ground
seedling	a young plant

Name: _____ Date: _____

Points of Confusion

Directions: Preview the text. Write words and ideas that might be confusing. Next, write notes about the meaning. Read the text and add to the notes.

Confusing Words and Ideas	Notes about the Meaning

Feature Help

Objectives

- Know and use various text features to locate key facts or information in a text.
- Explain how specific images contribute to and clarify a text.

Background Information

Students seem naturally drawn to the colorful pictures, charts, and diagrams in content-area texts. Helping them develop interpretative and inferential thinking about these text features supports reading comprehension. During content-area instruction, guide students to closely examine and integrate information from many sources, including pictures and other text features, prior to reading. This will help students formulate expectations about what they will learn and will support their comprehension of the text (McTigue and Flowers 2011).

Materials

- *Features Can Help* (page 129)
- text with some of the following: pictures with captions, charts, diagrams, time lines

Process

1. Prepare for the whole-group lesson by selecting a text with a variety of text features. Show the text to students, flipping through pages and pointing out the text features.

2. Explain that authors include a variety of text features in their work to help readers better understand written material. Lead a discussion about each text feature and the kind of information it provides. Display *Features Can Help*, and use it to make a class chart about the features and the information.

3. Give students a text and their own copies of *Features Can Help*. Ask students to identify the features in their text, then study each text feature and write what they learn from it. Ask students to predict what the text will be about based on the text features.

4. Have students read the text. After students read, discuss how previewing the text features helped them understand what they read.

Differentiation

Give additional support by working with students in a small group and focusing on one text feature at a time. Provide several different texts with the feature and have students find it in each text. Some students will benefit by working with partners to study text features and complete the *Features Can Help* activity sheet.

Name: _____ Date: _____

Features Can Help

Directions: Look at the text. List the text features you find. Write what you learned from them. Predict what the text is about.

Text Features
caption   time line   bold print   diagram

Text Feature	What I Learned

My prediction: _____

_____

Writing

The strategies in this section correspond with key competencies identified in *What the Science of Reading Says about Writing* (Jump and Wolfe 2023). These research-based instructional strategies will help teachers bridge the gap between the science of literacy instruction and classroom practice.

Strategy	Skills and Understandings Addressed			
	Genre Characteristics	Prewriting and Organization	Revise for Purpose	Grammar, Usage, and Mechanics
Pairing Texts and Graphic Organizers	■			
Mini Writes	■			
RAFT		■		
Framed Paragraphs		■		
Revision Discussion Prompts			■	
Growing Sentences			■	
Paragraph First Aid				■
Create a Sentence				■

The connection between reading and writing is complex and intricate, placing the act of reading as a necessary and crucial counterpart to writing. This reading-writing connection is obvious to most educators, yet reading and writing have traditionally been taught as separate subjects (Dewitz et al. 2020), and commonly, reading instruction takes precedence over writing. Teachers can face many obstacles when it comes to teaching writing: writing well and teaching it well take time and focus. In some states, standardized testing emphasizes reading and writing absent an explicit focus on writing in the curriculum. Additional obstacles include students' reading abilities, which can hamper their writing abilities and their motivation for writing. Increasingly however, educators are embracing a combined approach to reading and writing instruction, as they recognize the benefits of doing so (Dewitz et al. 2020; Graham and Hebert 2010). Teachers recognize that given the complex communication realities of the modern world, the ability to write well across a variety of mediums and genres is critical to academic and career success. They also acknowledge that reading and writing are reciprocal processes. Reading and reading instruction can improve the organization and quality of writing. Writing instruction can improve reading fluency and comprehension.

> Reading and writing are reciprocal processes. Reading and reading instruction can improve the organization and quality of writing. Writing instruction can improve reading fluency and comprehension.

These points underscore the importance of writing instruction as part of a comprehensive approach to reading and literacy instruction. The development of writing abilities begins early—the primary grades lay the foundation—and effective writing instruction through the elementary grades is critical for continued success in both reading and writing. Learning in one area enhances learning in the other. There is ample evidence to suggest that the processes are inseparable and that we should design our instruction considering these interrelationships. Fitzgerald and Shanahan (2000) describe this interrelationship when they propose that reading and writing are independent yet reciprocal processes that share common knowledge and skills, therefore what one learns in reading can be applied to writing and vice versa. Knowledge and skills are organized into four categories: *metaknowledge*: establishing a purpose, self-monitoring, self-evaluating; *domain knowledge*: vocabulary, topical/content knowledge; *text attributes*: mechanics, grammar, text structure; and *procedural knowledge*: knowing how to approach the writing task, constructing and generating meaning, analyzing, critiquing (Jouhar and Rupley 2020).

From a pedagogical perspective, a comprehensive review of the research supports the following recommendations (Graham et al. 2012b):

- Provide daily time for writing.
- Teach students the writing process, and teach students to write for a variety of purposes.
- Teach students to become fluent in handwriting/typing, spelling, and sentence construction.
- Create an engaged community of writers.

The Role of Purpose, Genre, and Process in Writing

Writing is a complex, cognitive, self-directed, goal-driven activity that communicates thoughts and ideas (Graham et al. 2012). As students progress through the elementary grades, writing should become an increasingly independent task. Knowledge and practice of the purpose of writing, the genres of writing, and the writing process facilitate independence and skill. Understanding purpose is key to effective writing as writers consider what they wish to share, the medium and genre appropriate for the task, and to whom they are writing. Students must have practice in writing for a variety of purposes, learning how to argue and persuade, convey information, respond to literature, share an experience, or tell stories for the purpose of entertaining an audience. Each of these purposes reflects the various genres of writing and each genre connects reading and writing skills differently, relying on a variety of skills and strategies in both unique and complementary ways.

The writing process includes planning, drafting, sharing, revising/editing, publishing, and reflection/evaluation. Effective writers use these components flexibly as guidelines and guideposts for accomplishing writing tasks. Research demonstrates that explicit instruction in each component of the writing process, in general, and related to specific genres, can help students develop as effective writers (Graham et al. 2012; Koster et al. 2015). Employing a model of gradual release during writing instruction is an important part of developing independent writers.

> Research demonstrates that explicit instruction in each component of the writing process, both in general and related to specific genres, can help students develop as effective writers.

The Writing Process

Writing for meaning and expressing oneself to others is intricate and complex work. Using the writing process helps the writer take a piece of writing from the beginning, or brainstorming, to the end, or the published piece. This process is especially important to follow as students write reports, essays, and other writing assignments. The writing process at the emergent writing level is usually conducted as a group, though on occasion it is done individually. Students in higher grades who have more familiarity with the writing process can complete it individually. There are different points to consider at each step of the writing process.

Prewriting

This is the phase during which all writing begins. At this stage, writers generate ideas, brainstorm topics, web ideas together, or talk and think about ideas. Teachers explain that students may get writing ideas from personal experiences, stories, pictures, television, websites, social media, and a variety of other sources.

This phase sets the foundation for a specific piece of writing. Students need to have a clear understanding of a writing assignment (i.e., the prompt) before they are expected to write or report on it. Before brainstorming or prewriting can begin, students need instruction on the genre or format (research report, journal entry, visual presentation, etc.), audience (the teacher, classmates, their families, the school community, etc.), and purpose (to explain, to persuade, to inform, etc.). These elements impact the types of information to brainstorm.

What does prewriting look like?

- analyzing the prompt
- researching a chosen topic, using print and digital sources
- analyzing the characteristics of the intended genre
- examining sample writing pieces
- discussing the topic with the teacher, a partner, or the class
- brainstorming ideas about the topic
- discussing the assessment tool
- creating a graphic organizer to organize ideas and the structure of the writing

Drafting

At the drafting stage of the writing process, students begin to put their ideas on paper. Students need to keep in mind the genre or format, audience, and purpose. For beginning writers, pictures and drawings are usually part of the composition. Teachers should encourage students to write as much as they can on their own throughout the writing process.

Some students struggle with writing in an orderly manner. Graphic organizers, notes, or outlines from the prewriting stage can help students sequence and organize their writing.

What does drafting look like?

- oral rehearsal of what will be written
- focusing on simply putting ideas on paper
- working fairly quickly
- leaving blank spaces for missing words
- approximating spelling
- using notes or graphic organizers to stay focused

Revising/Editing

This phase of writing consists of two parts: revising looks at the organization and structure of the writing, while editing looks at the mechanics of the writing. Students must understand how to do both. When revising, students analyze their writing for the required traits: sequencing words in a step-by-step process, descriptive language in a fictional story, or topic sentences and supporting details in a persuasive piece. When editing, students analyze their writing for correct spelling, grammar, and punctuation.

They also ask questions of their writing: *Does it make sense? Is anything out of order? Should anything be added or deleted?*

What do revising and editing look like?

- reading the piece aloud to confirm that it makes sense
- adding missing information
- deleting unnecessary, incorrect, or duplicate information
- proofreading for spelling, capitalization, grammar, and punctuation
- self-analysis by students
- conferences with peers or the teacher

Publishing

Publishing allows students to write for an authentic audience and celebrate their hard work. It occurs after the other steps are completed and the student is ready to produce the final copy, which can be handwritten or typed. The goal is to present the written information attractively so others can enjoy it.

What does publishing look like?

- creating a final copy
- adding illustrations, borders, a cover, and so on
- sharing orally
- publishing in a class book
- posting on a classroom website, a blog, a social media site, or another platform

Ensuring that students understand the purpose for crafting a piece of writing and the elements of the genre, along with consistently providing students time to work through the process of writing, will allow them to hone their craft. As they develop as writers, they will become better at expressing their thoughts and ideas within the different genres.

The Role of Conventions, Organization, and Expression in Writing

As discussed previously, when students have a firm command of the foundations of reading (decoding and fluency), they can better attend to comprehension of a text. Similarly with writing, when foundational skills are in place, more time and attention can be spent on the craft of writing (Graham et al. 2012). Strong foundations in phonological awareness, phonemic awareness, and phonics aid in the development of skillful sentence composition and the orthographic knowledge necessary for good writing. Vocabulary and morphology knowledge can give students freedom and flexibility over word choice and expression that can allow them to write more freely as opposed to struggling over the choice and spelling of specific words while composing. When these foundations have been laid, writing instruction can focus on the development and polishing of skilled writing, concentrating on generating increasingly complex and sophisticated sentences and interesting, well-organized writing.

Joan Sedita (2019) identifies five strands that contribute to skilled writing:

- **Critical thinking**—Critical thinking and executive functioning, awareness of the writing process, the use of background knowledge
- **Syntax**—How sentences work
- **Text structure**—Types of texts, paragraph structures, organizational patterns, linking and transition words
- **Writing craft**—Word choice, audience, and literary devices
- **Transcription**—Spelling, handwriting, and keyboarding

Effective instruction that supports organization, expression, and proper use of conventions includes the use of mentor texts, embedded writing tasks, and instruction in writing at the sentence level (Hochman and Wexler 2017; Tompkins 2018).

Encouraging Developing Writers

There are a variety of ways to teach students new ideas and to incorporate writing into the curriculum. Finding opportunities to weave together writing experiences and text is critical. In addition to teaching writers craft for its own sake, writing can be used to explain and communicate learning and understanding and as a response to reading. Many of the same practices of good readers are also done by good writers; they set goals, make predictions, make inferences, and read selectively. The more students write, the more skilled they will become in both reading and writing. Here are some characteristics of good writers that can inform instructional considerations for developing strong writers in your classroom:

- Writers write all the time. The more experience one has writing, the better writer one becomes. Learning to write takes practice and more practice!

- Writers read a lot. Reading provides a great model for writers as to what the finished product looks like. Students who read will know how to write better than those who do not.

- Writers are aware of correct spelling. These writers use all the resources available and understand the limitations of spell-check programs.

- Writers appreciate critiques and feedback. These writers have a "thick skin" and ask for input and suggestions from many different sources.

- Writers keep a record of their learning and ideas in journals or learning logs. These records can be used to store good writing ideas, document what is being learned, activate prior knowledge, and question what is being learned (Brozo and Simpson 2003; Fisher and Frey 2020). This can also help students avoid writer's block.

- Writers compose for a variety of purposes. Learning to write in a variety of formats makes for a well-rounded, experienced writer. Writers explore different types of writing formats.

- Writers read and edit other people's writing. Such writers look for opportunities to work with others to improve their writing. Peer editing groups are an excellent way to get feedback and reinforcement from peers. This feedback is important for the self-image of the writer (Gahn 1989). Editing others' work will also help students recognize writing errors, such as an off-topic response, a weak topic sentence, a lack of supporting detail, weak vocabulary, and errors in spelling or grammar.

- Writers think objectively. They are able to step back and really look at their writing.

- Writers read their work aloud! Many errors or additions are discovered when a student listens to the writing being read aloud.

The strategies that follow are designed to support the development of writers. They support flexible, generic structures, processes, and procedures intended to become a regular part of your writing instruction and writing routines.

Pairing Texts and Graphic Organizers

Objectives

- Produce clear and coherent writing in which the development, organization, and style are appropriate to task.

Background Information

To be successful in composing for a variety of purposes and audiences, students need to develop an awareness of genre conventions. To introduce writing in a new genre to young students, the first lesson should be analysis of the genre. It is valuable to use a children's book that highlights how a published author (mentor) has used the genre. This mentor text can bring text structure to life and help students learn about the organization, goals, and function of language in a specific genre (Brugar 2019; Herusatoto 2018; Kang 2020). It is also beneficial to pair a graphic organizer for the particular genre with the mentor text. Graphic organizers can assist students in creating a visual model of the genre being analyzed (Gallavan and Kottler 2007; Mercuri 2010). Once students are familiar with the characteristics of a specific genre through studying models, they can move through the writing process to compose their own texts in the genre.

Materials

- text that highlights a specific genre (e.g., narrative/description/sequence, informative/explanatory, cause and effect, opinion, or compare and contrast)
- graphic organizer that corresponds to the text genre (pages 140–149)

Process

1. Read aloud the entire text or a particular excerpt that highlights the genre.
2. Discuss the text, asking students what the text is telling the reader. Identify the genre and explore with students what the author's purpose might be in using the genre.
3. Distribute copies of the graphic organizer or reproduce it in chart form.
4. Reread the text to students, and think aloud while showing how to add information from the text to the graphic organizer.
5. Ask students to share additional information from the text that can be added to the graphic organizer.
6. When the graphic organizer is completed, discuss the information it shows.

7. Provide multiple opportunities for students to use the graphic organizer for a specific genre. Once students are familiar with the organizer, they can complete it independently.

Differentiation

Students may benefit from working in pairs or small groups to complete the graphic organizers.

Compare and Contrast *Example*

Title: Country Kid, City Kid

Jody   Ben

Alike

Can see
skyscrapers

Playground has
a fence

Shops at small
stores

Rides city bus
to school

Both play games

Both get mail

Both buy groceries

Both go to school

Can see fields
and farms

Plays on a big field

Shops at a big store

Rides school bus
to school

Name: _____ Date: _____

Compare and Contrast

Directions: On the lines, write the two things you are comparing and contrasting. Write your ideas in the Venn diagram.

Title: _____

_____   _____

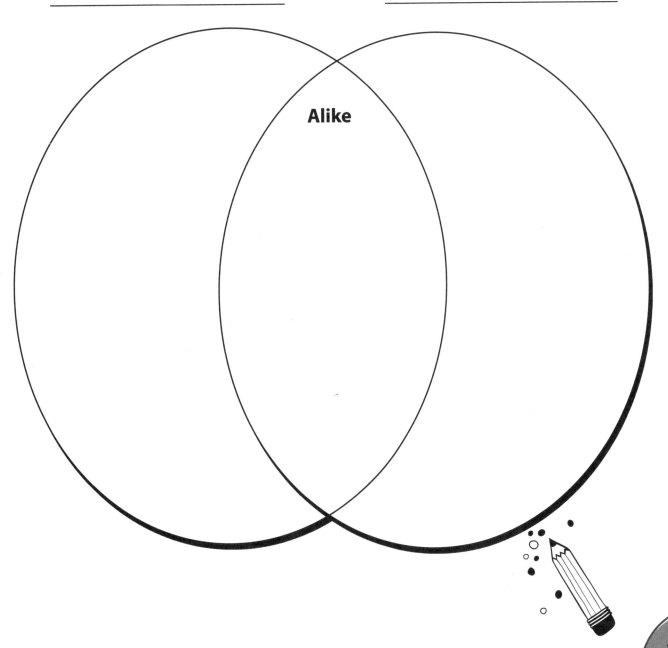

Alike

Sequence Example

Title: A Chair for My Mother

1. The girl and her mom save their money in a jar.

2. The jar got full and they had enough to buy a new chair.

3. They went shopping and tried lots of chairs.

4. They found the perfect chair and bought it.

Name: _____ Date: _____

Sequence

Directions: Write and draw events from the story in the order they happened.

Title: _____

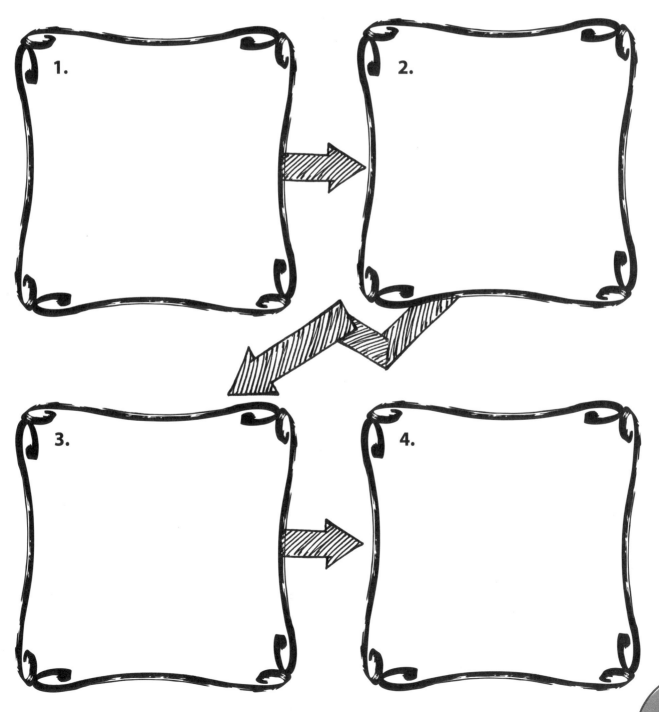

Description **Example**

Title: Charlotte's Web

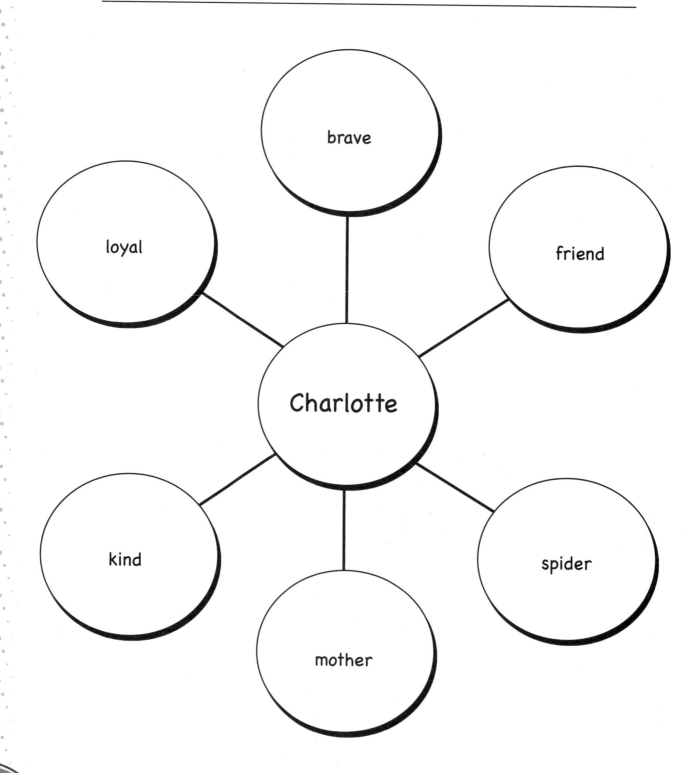

Name: _____ **Date:** _____

Description

Directions: In the center, write the topic. Around the topic, write describing words.

Title: _____

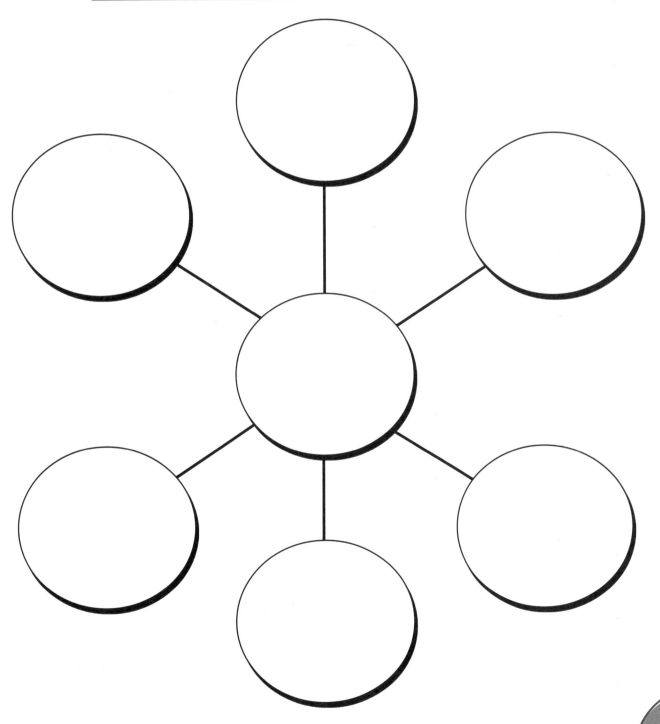

Cause and Effect *Example*

Title: Harry the Dirty Dog

Cause Why did something happen?		**Effect** What happened?
Harry heard the bath water.		He hid the scrub brush and ran away from home.
Harry played and got very dirty.		His family didn't recognize him.
The children gave Harry a bath.		His family recognized him and everyone was happy.

Cause and Effect

Directions: Write or draw causes and effects from the story.

Title: _____

Cause Why did something happen?		Effect What happened?
	→	
	→	
	→	

Main Idea and Details *Example*

Our Natural Resources

Air

People and animals breathe air to live.

Needs to be clean

Plants need air to grow.

Water

Helps plants grow

Animals and people need water to live.

All the water we have has always been on Earth.

Sunlight

Makes plants grow

Warms the earth

Melts the ice to make water

Name: _____ Date: _____

Main Idea and Details

Directions: On the top line, write the main idea. In the boxes, write details.

_____

Mini Writes

Objectives

- Write opinion pieces that introduce the topic, state an opinion, supply a reason for the opinion, and provide some sense of closure.
- Write informative/explanatory texts that name a topic, supply some facts about the topic, and provide some sense of closure.
- Write narratives that recount two or more appropriately sequenced events, include some details, use temporal words to signal event order, and provide some sense of closure.

Background Information

Learning to choose words carefully when writing can be a challenge for young writers with developing vocabularies. Add to that challenge the idea that each writing genre has its own specific vocabulary. "Identifying the genre provides a roadmap for the writer, with common organizational structures and features" (Jump and Wolfe 2023). Mini Writes help students learn about the genre and the corresponding genre-specific vocabulary and practice using them to complete a quick writing assignment.

Materials

- opinion, informative/explanatory, or narrative texts
- chart paper
- *My Mini Write* (page 152)
- highlighters

Process

1. Select the writing genre (opinion, informative/explanatory, narrative) that will be the focus of the lesson. This strategy can be repeated using a different genre each time.

2. Select at least one sample text of the genre you are going to study. Display and read the text with students. Ask students to identify keywords, terms, or phrases that move the writing along. These are the words, terms, and phrases that help the reader understand what is happening in the text. You may need to point out a few as examples before students are able to identify words on their own. As you read additional texts, students will start to see and identify keywords on their own.

3. Label chart paper with the genre, and make a list of all the keywords, terms, or phrases found in the text. See the example below for keywords. You and your students will be able to find additional key vocabulary as you explore texts.

4. Once you have a list of key vocabulary terms, display a copy of *My Mini Write*. Show students how to write the name of the genre and list keywords in the word bank. Ask students to use the words in their word banks to draft Mini Writes in the selected genre.

5. When students complete their writing, have them exchange papers with partners and read each others' drafts. Provide highlighters and ask students to highlight the key vocabulary words used in the drafts.

6. Display the charts showing genre-related vocabulary words in the classroom. Remind students to refer to them during future writing activities.

Differentiation

Some students may need to read multiple texts in a particular genre type before being able to identify and use key terms. You may wish to provide these students with their own copies of the texts and allow them to highlight key terms that have been listed on the class chart. When students are ready for an independent writing activity, help them select just a few keywords to use in their writing. Encourage advanced students to independently explore a new writing genre, find key terms, and use them to complete a Mini Write.

Genre Chart Example

	Opinion	Informative/ Explanatory	Narrative
Purpose	Convince or persuade	Give information or explain	Tell a story
Key Vocabulary	I think/I feel/I believe opinion one reason another reason for example finally as you can see	first, second, third to begin with another next then finally in conclusion	once upon a time in the beginning meanwhile suddenly at the same time the next day later

Name: _____ Date: _____

My Mini Write

Directions: Write the name of the genre. Write keywords in the word bank. Use the keywords to complete a mini write.

Genre: _____

```
┌─────────────────────────────────────────────┐
│                 Word Bank                     │
│                                               │
│                                               │
│                                               │
│                                               │
│                                               │
└─────────────────────────────────────────────┘
```

My Mini Write

_____

_____

_____

_____

_____

_____

RAFT

Objectives

- Produce clear and coherent writing in which the development, organization, and style are appropriate to task.

Background Information

RAFT stands for Role, Audience, Format, and Topic—the key ingredients of writing assignments (Dani, Litchfield, and Hallman-Thrasher 2018; Santa, Havens, and Valdes 1995). RAFT is a writing strategy to help students understand their roles as writers, the audience they will write for, and how to communicate their ideas effectively across varied formats and purposes for writing. Developing a sense of a purpose and audience in writing is key in effective communication. RAFT writing supports students in considering topics from multiple perspectives, thinking and writing creatively, and developing understanding of main ideas, coherence, and elaboration. RAFT can be implemented in any content area.

Materials

- mentor text
- *RAFT Planner* (page 155)

Process

1. Share a short mentor text with the class in which the elements of RAFT are clear and easy to determine. Lead students in a discussion to identify the following elements in the text:

   - Role: From whose perspective is the text written? (e.g., student, child, pet, tree, animal)

   - Audience: To whom is this author writing? (e.g., parent, owner, hikers, animal)

   - Format: What is the format of the writing? (e.g., letter, email, speech, ad)

   - Topic and strong verb: What is the writing about? What is the purpose of this communication? (strong verb to determine purpose and tone) (e.g., persuade, argue, complain, apologize, promise)

2. Explain to students that writers consider these RAFT elements before they write.

3. Display the *RAFT Planner*, and brainstorm ideas for each element with the class. Record students' ideas on the planner, modeling how to write responses to the RAFT prompts. Choose one set of prompts for students to use.

4. Have students practice writing to the chosen RAFT prompts. Students can work in small groups, in pairs, or independently.

Differentiation

Introduce each part of RAFT separately to allow students to develop command over one component before moving to the next. As students become more familiar with the strategy, teachers may provide more than one example for one of the elements to demonstrate how varying the elements can change the writing. For example, the prompt may share the same Role, Audience, and Topic, but students can choose from a variety of Formats.

RAFT Example

Role: a dog

Audience: the kid who owns him

Format: note

Topic and Strong Verb: pleads to spend more time playing together

Writing:

Hi Anna Banana,

We have been best friends for a long time. When you were small, we did everything together. I liked when we played catch in the backyard. My favorite time was our long walks around the block. Now you don't have time for me. Every day when you come home, I follow you and bark. But you ignore me! Take me on a walk, please. I love you.

Your BFF,
Sparky

Name: _____ Date: _____

RAFT Planner

Directions: Respond to the prompts. Use your answers to complete your writing on a separate sheet of paper.

R Role	
A Audience	
F Format	
T Topic and Strong Verb	

Framed Paragraphs

Objectives

- Produce clear and coherent writing in which the development, organization, and style are appropriate to task.

Background Information

A Framed Paragraph is a skeletal paragraph that includes strategically placed signal words that match the text structure (e.g., cause and effect, compare and contrast, sequencing) (Brozo and Simpson 2003). After using a graphic organizer as a scaffold to organize information, a Framed Paragraph provides students with support to convey the information using content-area language with appropriate syntax and structure (Cudd and Roberts 1989; Knipper and Duggan 2006). Framed Paragraphs can use different levels of signal words and can be modified as a single sentence based on learners' abilities.

Materials

- previously completed graphic organizer (see pages 140–149) based on text structure (opinion, narrative/description/sequence, informative/explanatory, cause and effect, or compare and contrast)
- Framed Paragraph (created by teacher, see examples on page 157)

Process

1. Create and display a Framed Paragraph based on the graphic organizer students have completed.

2. Model for students how to use information from the graphic organizer to complete the Framed Paragraph. Discuss and model how to reword ideas if needed so they will work in the sentence frames.

3. Distribute writing paper and have students use their graphic organizers to complete the paragraph on their own.

4. Have students read their paragraphs to partners to ensure the wording for each sentence makes sense.

Differentiation

Display examples of the completed Framed Paragraph for students to reference. Provide additional small-group support to students as they complete the Framed Paragraph to ensure they understand the process. After modeling one text structure, use graphic organizers and Framed Paragraphs to model other text structures.

Framed Paragraph Examples

Compare-and-Contrast

_____ and _____ are both _____. Both _____ and _____ have _____. _____ and _____ are alike because they both _____. _____ and _____ are different because _____. One difference between _____ and _____ is _____.

Lions and tigers are both animals. Both lions and tigers have fur. Lions and tigers are alike because they both have sharp teeth. Lions and tigers are alike because they both eat large animals. Lions and tigers are different because lions are one color and tigers have stripes. One difference between lions and tigers is that lions live with other lions, but tigers live alone. (Based on *Lions and Tigers* by Katy Pike, 2004)

Cause-and-Effect

The reason why _____ was because _____. If _____ hadn't _____, then _____. Since _____, _____. _____ explains why _____.

The reason why the woman was late was because of the rain coming down. If the rain hadn't come down, then the boy wouldn't have splashed the girl. Since the rain came down, people argued. The rain explains why everyone was acting weird. (Based on *The Rain Came Down* by David Shannon, 2000)

Sequence

Here is how a _____ grows. First, a _____ is _____. Next, the _____. Then, the _____. Finally, _____.

Here is how a seed grows. First, a seed is planted. Next, roots grow in the ground. Then, leaves begin to grow. Finally, the plant is above the ground. (Based on *How Plants Grow* by Dona Herwick Rice, 2012)

Descriptive

_____ can be described in many ways. One way to describe _____ is _____. _____ is _____ because _____. Another way to describe _____ is _____. _____ is _____ because _____. Finally, _____ is _____. _____ is the best description because _____.

Charlotte can be described in many ways. One way to describe Charlotte is kind. Charlotte is kind because she tries to save Wilbur. Another way to describe Charlotte is a friend. Charlotte is a friend because she creates words in her web to save Wilbur. Finally, Charlotte is brave. Brave is the best description because Charlotte knows she can't go back to the farm with Wilbur. (Based on *Charlotte's Web* by E. B. White, 1952)

Revision Discussion Prompts

Objectives

- With guidance and support from adults and peers, focus on a topic and strengthen writing as needed by revising and editing.

Background Information

Revision may be the most rigorous and challenging part of the writing process. Often students, and sometimes teachers, combine revision and editing, but they are distinct processes. Revision is where the ideas from prewriting and composing come to life and are clarified and distilled. During revision, students apply and refine their knowledge of structure, syntax, and word choice. A checklist is an excellent tool to support student independence with the process (Lopas et al. 2021). This strategy provides students with a scaffold to participate in discussions.

Materials

- drafts of students' writing ready for revision
- *Revision Discussion Prompts* (page 159)

Process

1. Distribute *Revision Discussion Prompts* to students. Discuss each of the main components of strong writing:
   - The title matches the writing.
   - The introduction is interesting.
   - Details help the reader create a picture in their mind.
   - The ending sums up the writing.
   - The writing is for specific readers.
2. Tell students they will use the prompts to discuss their writing with partners.
3. The first student reads their draft aloud. Partners think about and discuss the writing and the prompts. Students switch roles to discuss the second student's writing.
4. Provide time for students to revise their writing based on their partner discussions.

Differentiation

Gather a small group of students who need additional support and take turns reading their drafts and going through the prompts. When students are ready, they can select elements to focus on and participate in a conversation (e.g., students may choose to work on conclusions).

Name: _____ Date: _____

Revision Discussion Prompts

Directions: Read the writing. Circle your response. Explain your thoughts, and give ideas the writer may want to try.

Your Response	Feedback to Make It Better
1. The title matches the writing. yes needs work	
2. The introduction is interesting. yes needs work	
3. Details help the reader create pictures in their mind. yes needs work	
4. The ending sums up the writing. yes needs work	
5. The writing is for specific readers. yes needs work	

Growing Sentences

Objectives

- Produce and expand complete simple and compound sentences in response to prompts.

Background Information

Young writers tend to compose simplistic sentences that do not provide many details. Basic sentences tend to follow the article, noun, verb pattern (e.g., *The boy ran.*). Teaching students how to increase the complexity of their sentences has been shown to increase the quality of students' writing (Graham and Perin 2007). In the early grades, teachers can aid students in growing their sentences by providing prompts that will guide students to add important details and offer more information to the reader. Growing Sentences provides a scaffold for young students as it draws on their oral language production to increase the complexity of their written sentence production.

Materials

- chart paper
- *Growing Sentences Flower* (page 162)
- recent pieces of students' writing

Process

1. Draw the *Growing Sentences Flower* graphic organizer on chart paper.

2. Provide a simple sentence for the class to expand as a group (e.g., *The boy ran.*).

3. Model how to answer the questions on the petals with ideas that provide more details.
   - How did the boy run? (e.g., *fast, slowly, quickly, happily*)
   - Where did the boy run? (e.g., *on the playground, outside, on the field, at the beach*)
   - When did the boy run? (e.g., *after school, on Saturday, in the summer, at noon*)
   - Why did the boy run? (e.g., *to chase his dog, to get home, to steal second base, to jump in the waves*)

4. Work with the students to create expanded sentences by using the answers to the prompts (e.g., *The boy ran quickly at the beach in the summer to jump in the waves.*).

5. Distribute copies of *Growing Sentences Flower* to students. Have each student select a sentence from a recent piece of their own writing. Have students use their activity sheets to create expanded sentences.

Differentiation

You might only address one prompt a day (e.g., just the *when* or *why*). Once you have demonstrated how to answer each prompt, you can take students through the production of new sentences. After that, students can complete the activity sheet on their own.

Name: _____ Date: _____

✳ Growing Sentences Flower ✳

Directions: Write a sentence. Then, answer the questions. Use the answers to grow your sentence. Write the new sentence.

My sentence: _____

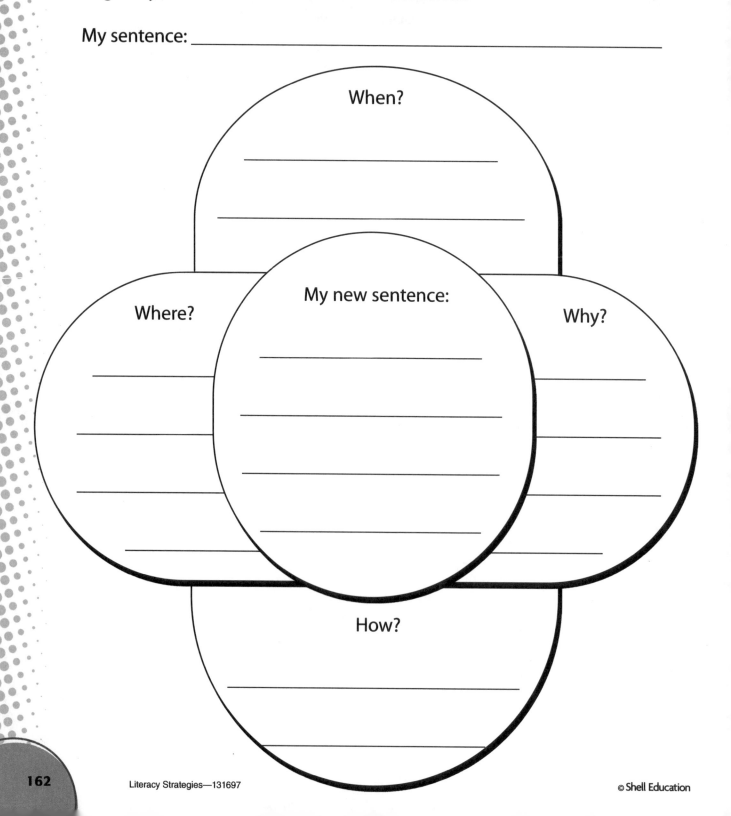

When?

_____

_____

Where?

_____

_____

_____

My new sentence:

_____

_____

_____

_____

Why?

_____

_____

_____

How?

_____

_____

Paragraph First Aid

Objectives

- Use standard English conventions, including capitalization, punctuation, and spelling when writing.

Background Information

Knowledge of and proper use of writing mechanics are essential for good writing. Not only do writing mechanics assist the writer in being clear, they also make it easier for the reader to understand what has been written. To learn to write for real purposes (Graham 2019), students need to consistently use good writing mechanics. Paragraph First Aid reinforces writing mechanics, then engages students in using the mechanics to fix a paragraph, extending their learning to their ongoing writing. This reinforcement supports students in applying writing mechanics more consistently.

Materials

- paragraph with correct mechanics; a paragraph with proper names and words in a series is best
- paragraph with incorrect mechanics
- *First Aid* (page 165) copies on card stock
- small storage bags

Process

1. Display the correctly written paragraph. Ask students to read the paragraph to themselves and then read it aloud together. Discuss how the capitalization and punctuation help make the paragraph easy to read and understand.

2. Cut out the bandages from a copy of the *First Aid* page and use a document camera to show them to students. Explain that just as they use bandages to help when they get hurt, paragraphs need help to be easy to read. Tell students the bandages have ways to help make paragraphs easier to understand.

3. Read the text on one bandage, and ask students to identify where in the paragraph that direction was followed. Repeat this for each bandage, discussing how following the directions helps the paragraph.

4. Distribute *First Aid,* and have students cut out the bandages. Display the paragraph with errors. Distribute writing paper and tell students to use the bandages to check the paragraph and rewrite it correctly.

5. When students finish correcting the paragraph, have them trade papers with partners. Encourage partners to use their bandages to check one another's work.

6. Have students store the bandages in small bags. During future writing activities, remind the students to use the bandages to check their work.

Differentiation

Some students may need to work on a few of the mechanics principles at a time. Highlight only a few sentences of the text and give them two bandages to use. Encourage them to find and fix those errors in the highlighted sentences. For additional support, draw a picture or example on the back of each bandage. Encourage advanced students to write short stories and then use the bandages to check their mechanics.

Name: _____ Date: _____

First Aid

Directions: Cut out the bandages. Follow the directions to check and fix your writing.

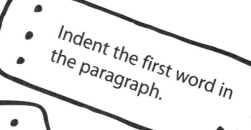

Indent the first word in the paragraph.

End every sentence with punctuation.

Capitalize the first word in every sentence.

Capitalize names of people.

Leave spaces between words.

Use commas between a series of words.

Start a new paragraph on a new line.

Create a Sentence

Objectives

- Use common, proper, and possessive nouns. Use verbs to convey a sense of past, present, and future. Use frequently occurring adjectives. Use frequently occurring prepositions.

- Produce, expand, and rearrange complete simple and compound sentences.

Background Information

Create a Sentence focuses on parts of speech and their roles in sentences and helps young writers learn how to expand sentences by including adjectives and adverbs. Sentence-expansion lessons help students create stronger, more interesting sentences (Knight 2017). This strategy begins with a noun and adjectives; then students add verbs, adverbs, and prepositions that are related to the noun to form sentences.

Materials

- *Create a Sentence* (page 169)
- sticky notes

Process

1. Project a copy of *Create a Sentence* (or recreate it on chart paper).

2. Select a noun, and write it in the second column (e.g., *dog*).

3. Ask students for adjectives to describe a dog, and write them in the first column (e.g., *funny, hungry, hairy*).

4. Ask students to provide related verbs, and add them to the third column (e.g., *ran, jumped, barked*).

5. Elicit adverbs—"how" words—that describe the verbs, and add them to the fourth column (e.g., *lazily, sloppily, quickly*).

6. Ask students for "where" words, and add them to the prepositional phrases in the final column (e.g., *outside, over the fence*).

7. Lead the class in creating sentences by using a word from each column in the chart. Invite students to come up and place sticky notes on a word or phrase in each column to create the sentences.

8. Repeat the activity several times, beginning with a different noun each time.

9. Distribute copies of *Create a Sentence*, and have students complete them independently or with partners.

Differentiation

Students may need additional instruction on the parts of speech. Using different colors to add words to the different columns (for example, red for adjectives, black for nouns, green for verbs, blue for adverbs, and orange for prepositions) will support students in putting sentences together. For struggling students, you may wish to build the chart by adding only one word or phrase to each column, going from a simple sentence to a complex one. Advanced students can write sentences independently in their journals using the chart and then read them to partners.

Create a Sentence Example

Adjective Describe the noun.	Noun Person, place, or thing	Verb Action	Adverb Describe the action.	Prepositional Phrase Where or when?	
funny		played	lazily	outside	
hungry	dog	jumped	happily	over the fence	
sleepy		barked	excitedly	at the park	
playful		sat	playfully	inside	

My Sentence: The sleepy dog sat lazily inside.

Create a Sentence

Directions: Write a noun. Write words in the other columns. Write a sentence.

Adjective Describe the noun.	Noun Person, place, or thing	Verb Action	Adverb Describe the action.	Prepositional Phrase Where or when?

My Sentence:

REFERENCES

Adams, Marilyn. 1994. *Beginning to Read: Thinking and Learning About Print*. Cambridge: MIT Press.

———. 2011. "The Relation Between Alphabetic Basics, Word Recognition, and Reading." In *What Research Has to Say About Reading Instruction*, 4th edition, edited by S. Jay Samuels and Alan E. Farstrup, 4–24. Newark, DE: International Reading Association.

Almasi, Janice F., and Susan J. Hart. 2018. "Best Practices in Narrative Text Comprehension Instruction." In *Best Practice in Literacy Instruction*, 6th edition, edited by Lesley Mandel Morrow and Linda B. Gambrell, 221–249. New York: Guilford.

Anderson, Richard Chase, and P. David Pearson. 1984. "A Schema-Theoretic View of Basic Processes in Reading Comprehension." In *Handbook of Reading Research*, edited by P. David Pearson, with Rebecca Barr, Michael L. Kamil, and Peter Mosenthal, 255–291. New York: Routledge.

Anderson, Richard C., and William E. Nagy. 1992. "The Vocabulary Conundrum." *American Educator* 16 (4): 14–18, 44–47.

Armbruster, Bonnie B., Fran Lehr, and Jean Osborn. 2010. *Put Reading First: The Research Building Blocks for Teaching Children to Read: Kindergarten through Grade 3*. 3rd edition. Washington, DC: National Institute for Literacy.

Baker, Linda, and Ann L. Brown. 1984. "Metacognitive Skills and Reading." In *Handbook of Reading Research*, edited by P. David. Pearson, Michael L. Kamil, Peter B. Mosenthal, and Rebecca Barr, 353–394. New York: Longman.

Barnes, Douglas, and Frankie Todd. 1995. *Communication and Learning Revisited*. Portsmouth, NH: Heinemann.

Baumann, James F., and Michael F. Graves. 2010. "What Is Academic Vocabulary?" *Journal of Adolescent & Adult Literacy* 54 (1): 4–12. doi.org/10.1598/jaal.54.1.1.

Bear, Donald R., Marcia Invernizzi, Shane Templeton, and Francine Johnston. 2020. *Words Their Way: Word Study for Phonics, Vocabulary, and Spelling Instruction*. 7th edition. Upper Saddle River, NJ: Pearson.

Beck, Isabel, Margaret G. McKeown, and Linda Kucan. 2002. *Bringing Words to Life: Robust Vocabulary Instruction*. New York: Guilford.

Bhattacharya, Alpana, and Linnea C. Ehri. 2004. "Graphosyllabic Analysis Helps Adolescent Struggling Readers Read and Spell Words." *Journal of Learning Disabilities* 37 (4): 331–348. doi.org/10.1177/00222194040370040501.

Brozo, William G., and Michele L. Simpson. 2003. *Readers, Teachers, Learners: Expanding Literacy Across the Content Areas.* 4th edition. Upper Saddle River, NJ: Merrill.

Brugar, Kristy A. 2019. "Inquiry By the Book: Using Children's Nonfiction as Mentor Texts for Inquiry." *The Social Studies* 110 (4): 155–160.

Cabell, Sonia Q., and HyeJin Hwang. 2020. "Building Content Knowledge to Boost Comprehension in the Primary Grades." *Reading Research Quarterly* 55 (S1): S99–S107. doi.org/10.1002/rrq.338.

Cervetti, Gina N., Tanya S. Wright, and HyeJin Hwang. 2016. "Conceptual Coherence, Comprehension, and Vocabulary Acquisition: A Knowledge Effect?" *Reading and Writing* 29 (4): 761–779. doi.org/10.1007/s11145-016-9628-x.

Cromley, Jennifer G., and Roger Azevedo. 2007. "Testing and Refining the Direct and Inferential Mediation Model of Reading Comprehension." *Journal of Educational Psychology* 99 (2): 311–325. doi.org/10.1037/0022-0663.99.2.311.

Cudd, Evelyn T., and Leslie Roberts. 1989. "Using Writing to Enhance Content Area Learning in the Primary Grades." *The Reading Teacher* 42 (6): 392–404.

Dani, Danielle, Erin Litchfield, and Allyson Hallman-Thrasher. 2018. "Creative Assessments: Using RAFT Writing to Assess Students in a Course on Motion." *The Science Teacher* 85 (5): 46–53.

Dewitz, Peter, Michael Graves, Bonnie Graves, and Connie Juel. 2020. *Teaching Reading in the 21st Century: Motivating All Learners.* 6th edition. Saddle River, NJ: Pearson.

Doyle, Brooke Graham, and Wendie Bramwell. 2006. "Promoting Emergent Literacy and Social-Emotional Learning through Dialogic Reading." *The Reading Teacher* 59 (6): 554–64. jstor.org/stable/20204388.

Duke, Nell K., and Kelly B. Cartwright. 2021. "The Science of Reading Progresses: Communicating Advances Beyond the Simple View of Reading." *Reading Research Quarterly* (Special Issue) 56 (S1): S25–S44. doi.org/10.1002/rrq.411.

Duke, Nell K., and P. David Pearson. 2002. "Effective Practices for Developing Reading Comprehension." In *What Research Has to Say About Reading Instruction*, 3rd edition, edited by Alan E. Farstrup and S. Jay Samuels, 205–242. Newark, DE: International Reading Association.

Duke, Nell K., Alessandra E. Ward, and P. David Pearson. 2021. "The Science of Reading Comprehension Instruction." *The Reading Teacher* 74 (6): 663–672. doi.org/10.1002/trtr.1993.

Dunlap, Carmen Zuñiga, and Evelyn Marino Weisman. 2006. *Helping English Language Learners Succeed.* Huntington Beach, CA: Shell Education.

Durkin, Dolores. 1978. "What Classroom Observations Reveal About Reading Comprehension." *Reading Research Quarterly* 14 (4), 481–553. Newark, DE: International Reading Association.

Ehri, Linnea C. 1987. "Learning to Read and Spell Words." *Journal of Reading Behavior* 19 (1): 5–31.

———. 1992. "Reconceptualizing the Development of Sight Word Reading and Its Relationship to Recoding." In *Reading Acquisition*, edited by Philip B. Gough, Linnea C. Ehri, and Rebecca Treiman, 107–143. Hillsdale, NJ: Erlbaum.

———. 1998. "Grapheme-Phoneme Knowledge Is Essential for Learning to Read Words in English." In *Word Recognition in Beginning Literacy*, edited by Jamie L. Metsala and Linnea C. Ehri, 3–40. Mahwah, NJ: Erlbaum.

———. 2005. "Learning to Read Words: Theory, Findings and Issues." *Scientific Studies of Reading* 9 (2): 167–188.

———. 2014. "Orthographic Mapping in the Acquisition of Sight Word Reading, Spelling Memory, and Vocabulary Learning." *Scientific Studies of Reading* 18 (1): 5–21. doi.org/10.1080/10888438.2013.819356.

———. 2020. "The Science of Learning to Read Words: A Case for Systematic Reading Instruction." *Reading Research Quarterly* 55: S45–S60.

Ehri, Linnea C., Simone R. Nunes, Steven A. Stahl, and Dale M. Willows. 2001. "Systematic Phonics Instruction Helps Students Learn to Read: Evidence from the National Reading Panel's Meta-Analysis." *Review of Educational Research* 71 (3): 393–447. doi.org/10.3102/00346543071003393.

Farrell, Linda, Michael Hunter, and Tina Osenga. 2019. "A New Model for Teaching High-Frequency Words." *Reading Rockets*. readingrockets.org/article/new-model-teaching-high-frequency-words.

Fessel, Elizabeth, and Pamela Kennedy. 2019. "Teaching Sight Words According to Science." Ohio Department of Education Literacy Academy. education.ohio.gov/getattachment/Topics/Learning-in-Ohio/Literacy/Striving-Readers-Comprehensive-Literacy-Grant/Literacy-Academy/2-07-Teaching-Sight-Words-According-to-Science.pdf.

Fisher, Douglas, and Nancy Frey. 2008. *Word Wise and Content Rich, Grades 7–12: Five Essential Steps to Teaching Academic Vocabulary*. Portsmouth, NH: Heinemann.

———. 2020. *Improving Adolescent Literacy: Content Area Strategies at Work*. 5th edition. Upper Saddle River, NJ: Pearson.

Fitzgerald, Jill, and Timothy Shanahan. 2000. "Reading and Writing Relations and Their Development." *Educational Psychologist* 35 (1): 39–50. doi.org/10.1207/s15326985ep3501_5.

Gahn, Shelley Mattson. 1989. "A Practical Guide for Teaching Writing in the Content Areas." *Journal of Reading* 32 (6): 525–531.

Gallavan, Nancy P., and Ellen Kottler. 2007. "Eight Types of Graphic Organizers for Empowering Social Studies Students and Teachers." *The Social Studies* 98 (3): 117–128.

Goswami, Usha C. 2008. *Cognitive Development: The Learning Brain*. Hove, UK: Psychology Press.

Gough, Philip B., Connie Juel, and Diane Roper-Schneider. 1983. "Code and Cipher: A Two-Stage Conception of Initial Reading Acquisition." In *Searches for Meaning in Reading /Language Processing and Instruction*, edited by J. A. Niles and L. A. Harris, 207–211. Rochester, NY: National Reading Conference.

Gough, Philip B., and William E. Tunmer. 1986. "Decoding, Reading, and Reading Disability." *Remedial and Special Education* 7 (1): 6–10.

Gourgey, Annette F. 1998. "Metacognition in Basic Skills Instruction." *Instructional Science* 26 (1/2): 81–96. Philadelphia: Kluwer Academic Publishers. doi.org/10.1023/a:1003092414893.

Graham, Steve. 2019. "Changing How Writing Is Taught." *Review of Research in Education* 43: 277–303.

———. 2020. "The Sciences of Reading and Writing Must Become More Fully Integrated." *Reading Research Quarterly* 55 (S1): 5–S44. doi.org/10.1002/rrq.332.

Graham, Steve, Alisha Bollinger, Carol Booth Olson, Catherine D'Aoust, Charles MacArthur, Deborah McCutchen, Natalie and Olinghouse. 2012a. *Teaching Elementary School Students to Be Effective Writers: A Practice Guide* (NCEE 20124058). Washington, DC: National Center for Education Evaluation and Regional Assistance, Institute of Education Sciences, U.S. Department of Education. Retrieved from ies.ed.gov/ncee/wwc/publications_reviews.aspx#pubsearch.

Graham, Steve, and Michael Hebert. 2010. *Writing to Read: Evidence for How Writing Can Improve*. A Carnegie Corporation Time to Act Report. Washington, DC: Alliance for Excellent Education.

Graham, Steve, Debra McKeown, Sharlene Kiuhara, and Karen R. Harris. 2012b. "A Meta-Analysis of Writing Instruction for Students in the Elementary Grades." *Journal of Educational Psychology* 104 (4): 879–896. doi.org/10.1037/a0029185.

Graham, Steve, and Dolores Perin. 2007. "A Meta-Analysis of Writing Instruction for Adolescent Students." *Journal of Educational Psychology* 99 (3): 445–476. doi.org/10.1037/0022-0663.99.3.445.

Graves, Michael F., and Susan Watts-Taffe. 2008. "For the Love of Words: Fostering Word Consciousness in Young Readers." *The Reading Teacher* 62 (3): 185–193.

Greenwood, Scott C., and Kevin Flanigan. 2007. "Overlapping Vocabulary and Comprehension: Context Clues Complement Semantic Gradients." *The Reading Teacher* 61 (3): 249–254.

Hacker, Douglas J., John Dunlosky, and Arthur C. Graesser. 1998. *Metacognition in Educational Theory and Practice*. Mahwah, NJ: Erlbaum.

Halliday, M. A. K. 1975. *Learning How to Mean: Explorations in the Development of Language*. London: Edward Arnold.

Hattie, John. 2009. *Visible Learning: A Synthesis of Over 800 Meta-Analyses Relating to Achievement*. New York: Routledge.

Herusatoto, Hesthi. 2018. "Mentor Texts: Models to Improve False Beginners' Writing Skills." *Ethical Lingua: Journal of Language Teaching and Literature* 5 (2): 123–138.

Hirsch, E. D. 2006. "Building Knowledge: The Case for Bringing Content into the Language Arts Block and for a Knowledge-Rich Curriculum Core for All Children." *American Educator*, Spring 2006. American Federation of Teachers. aft.org/periodical /american-educator/spring-2006/building-knowledge.

Hochman, Judith C., and Natalie Wexler. 2017. "One Sentence at a Time: The Need for Explicit Instruction in Teaching Students to Write Well." *American Educator,* Summer 2017. American Federation of Teachers. aft.org/ae/summer2017/hochman-wexler.

Hollie, Sharroky. 2018. *Culturally and Linguistically Responsive Teaching and Learning, Second Edition*. Huntington Beach, CA: Shell Education.

Hoover, Wesley A., and Philip B. Gough. 1990. "The Simple View of Reading." *Reading and Writing: An Interdisciplinary Journal* 2 (2): 127–160. doi.org/10.1007/BF00401799.

Hoover, Wesley A., and William E. Tunmer. 2018. "The Simple View of Reading: Three Assessments of Its Adequacy." *Remedial and Special Education* 39 (5): 304–312. doi.org/10.1177/0741932518773154.

———. 2020. *The Cognitive Foundations of Reading and Its Acquisition: A Framework with Applications Connecting Teaching and Learning (Literacy Studies)*. London: Springer.

———. 2022. "The Primacy of Science in Communicating Advances in the Science of Reading." *Reading Research Quarterly* (57) 2: 399–408. doi.org/10.1002/rrq.446.

Horton, Phillip B., Andrew A. McConney, Michael Gallo, Amanda L. Woods, Gary J. Senn, and Denis Hamelin. 1993. "An Investigation of the Effectiveness of Concept Mapping as an Instructional Tool." *Science Education* 77 (1): 95–111. doi.org/10.1002 /sce.3730770107.

Hoyt, Linda. 2002. *Make It Real: Strategies for Success with Informational Texts*. Portsmouth, NH: Heinemann.

Hulit, Lloyd M., Merle R. Howard, and Kathleen R. Fahey. 2018. *Born to Talk: An Introduction to Speech and Language Development.* 7th edition. Boston, MA: Allyn and Bacon.

Jouhar, Mohammed R., and William H. Rupley. 2020. "The Reading–Writing Connection based on Independent Reading and Writing: A Systematic Review." *Reading & Writing Quarterly* 37 (2): 136–156. doi.org/10.1080/10573569.2020.1740632.

Jump, Jennifer, and Robin D. Johnson. 2023. *What the Science of Reading Says about Word Recognition.* Huntington Beach, CA: Shell Education.

Jump, Jennifer, and Kathleen Kopp. 2023. *What the Science of Reading Says about Reading Comprehension and Content Knowledge.* Huntington Beach, CA: Shell Education.

Jump, Jennifer, and Hillary Wolfe. 2023. *What the Science of Reading Says about Writing.* Huntington Beach, CA: Shell Education.

Kamil, Michael L., Geoffrey D. Borman, Janice Dole, Cathleen C. Kral, Terry Salinger, and Joseph Torgesen. 2008. *Improving Adolescent Literacy: Effective Classroom and Intervention Practices: A Practice Guide* (NCEE #2008-4027). Washington, DC: National Center for Education Evaluation and Regional Assistance, Institute of Education Sciences, U.S. Department of Education.

Kang, Eun Young. 2020. "Using Model Texts as a Form of Feedback in L2 Writing." *System* 89: 102196. doi.org/10.1016/j.system.2019.102196.

Keesey, Susan, Moira Konrad, and Laurice M. Joseph. 2015. "Word Boxes Improve Phonemic Awareness, Letter-Sound Correspondences, and Spelling Skills of At-Risk Kindergartners." *Remedial and Special Education* 36 (3): 167–180.

Kelley, Michelle, and Nicki Clausen-Grace. 2008. "From Picture Walk to Text Feature Walk: Guiding Students to Strategically Preview Informational Text." *Journal of Content Area Reading* 7 (1).

Kintsch, Walter. 1988. "The Role of Knowledge in Discourse Comprehension: A Construction-Integration Model." *Psychological Review* 95 (2): 163–82. doi.org/10.1037/0033-295x.95.2.163.

Knight, Jennifer. 2017. "Sentence Expansion Lessons Helps Students Create Stronger, More Interesting Sentences." (blog) *Iowa Reading Research Center.* April 25, 2017. iowareadingresearch.org/blog/sentence-expanding.

Knipper, Kathy J., and Timothy J. Duggan. 2006. "Writing to Learn across the Curriculum: Tools for Comprehension in Content Area Classes." *The Reading Teacher* 59 (5): 462–470.

Koster, Monica, Elena Tribushinina, Peter F. de Jong, Huub van den Bergh. 2015. "Teaching Children to Write: A Meta-Analysis of Writing Intervention Research." *Journal of Writing Research* 7 (2): 249–274. doi.org/10.17239/jowr-2015.07.02.2.

Krashen, Stephen. 2009. "81 Generalizations about Free Voluntary Reading." IATEFL Young Learner and Teenager Special Interest Group Publication. successfulenglish.com /wp-content/uploads/2010/01/81-Generalizations-about-FVR-2009.pdf.

Kress, Jacqueline E., and Edward B. Fry. 2016. *The Reading Teacher's Book of Lists*. 6th edition. San Francisco: Jossey-Bass.

Lapp, Diane, James Flood, and Nancy Farnan, eds. 2008. *Content Area Reading and Learning: Instructional Strategies*. 3rd edition. Boston: Allyn and Bacon.

LeVasseur, Valerie Marciarille, Paul Macaruso, and Donald Shankweiler. 2008. "Promoting Gains in Reading Fluency: A Comparison of Three Approaches." *Reading and Writing* 21 (3): 205–230. doi.org/10.1007/s11145-007-9070-1.

Lopas, Courtney M., Vassiliki (Vicky) I. Zygouris-Coe, Rebeca A. Grysko, and Su Gao. 2021. "Writing to Learn in Science: Accommodations to Support English-Language Learners' Writing Skills and Science Content Learning in Grade 5." *The Reading Teacher* 74 (5): 617–630. doi:10.1002/trtr.1979.

McConnell, Suzanne. 1993. "Talking Drawings: A Strategy for Assisting Learners." *Journal of Reading* 36 (4): 260–269.

McTigue, Erin M., and Amanda C. Flowers. 2011. "Science Visual Literacy: Learners' Perceptions and Knowledge of Diagrams." *The Reading Teacher* 64 (8): 578–589.

Mercuri, Sandra P. 2010. "Using Graphic Organizers as a Tool for the Development of Scientific Language." *GIST Education and Learning Research Journal* (November): 30–49.

Moats, Louisa C. 2020. "Teaching Reading Is Rocket Science." *American Educator*, Summer 2020. aft.org/ae/summer2020/moats.

Morrow, Lesley Mandel. 2003. "Motivating Lifelong Voluntary Readers." In *Handbook of Research on Teaching the English Language Arts*, edited by James Flood, Diane Lapp, James R. Squire, and Julie M. Jenson, 857–867. Mahwah, NJ: Erlbaum.

Mountain, Lee. 2015. "Recurrent Prefixes, Roots, and Suffixes: A Morphemic Approach to Disciplinary Literacy." *Journal of Adolescent and Adult Literacy* 58 (7): 561–567.

Nagy, William E., and Richard C. Anderson. 1984. "How Many Words Are There in Printed School English?" *Reading Research Quarterly* 19 (3): 304–330. doi.org/10.2307/747823.

Nagy, William E., and Judith A. Scott. 2000. "Vocabulary Processing." In *Handbook of Reading Research*, Vol. III, edited by Michael L., Kamil, Peter B. Mosenthal, P. David Pearson, and Rebecca Barr, 269–274. Mahwah, NJ: Erlbaum.

National Early Literacy Panel. 2008. *Developing Early Literacy: Report of the National Early Literacy Panel: A Scientific Synthesis of Early Literacy Development and Implications for Intervention.* Jessup, MD: National Institute for Literacy with National Center for Family Literacy.

National Reading Panel (U.S.) and National Institute of Child Health and Human Development (U.S.). 2000. *Report of the National Reading Panel: Teaching Children to Read: An Evidence-based Assessment of the Scientific Research Literature on Reading and Its Implications for Reading Instructio*n. Bethesda: U.S. Dept. of Health and Human Services, Public Health Service, National Institutes of Health, National Institute of Child Health and Human Development.

Nesbit, John C., and Olusola O. Adesope. 2006. "Learning with Concept and Knowledge Maps: A Meta-Analysis." *Review of Educational Research* 76 (3): 413–448. doi:10.3102/00346543076003413.

Neuman, Susan B., Tanya Kaefer, and Ashley Pinkham. 2014. "Building Background Knowledge." *Reading Teacher* 68 (2): 145–148. jstor.org/stable/24573715.

Palincsar, Annemarie Sullivan, and Deborah A. Brown. 1987. "Enhancing Instructional Time Through Attention to Metacognition." *Journal of Learning Disabilities* 20 (2): 66–75. Thousand Oaks, CA: SAGE Publications. doiorg/10.1177 /002221948702000201.

Paris, Scott G., Marjorie Y. Lipson, and Karen K. Wixson. 1983. "Becoming a Strategic Reader." *Contemporary Educational Psychology* 8 (3): 293–316. doi.org/10.1016/0361 -476x(83)90018-8.

Perfetti, Charles, and Joseph Stafura. 2013. "Word Knowledge in a Theory of Reading Comprehension." *Scientific Studies of Reading* 18 (1): 22–37. doi.org/10.1080/10888438 .2013.827687.

Pressley, Michael, and Peter Afflerbach. 1995. *Verbal Protocols of Reading: The Nature of Constructively Responsive Reading.* New York: Routledge.

Pressley, Michael, John G. Borkowski, and Wolfgang Schneider. 1987. "Cognitive Strategies: Good Strategy Users Coordinate Metacognition and Knowledge." *Annals of Child Development* 4: 89–129.

Pressley, Michael, Sara E. Dolezal, Lisa M. Raphael, Lindsey Mohan, Alysia D. Roehrig, and Kristen Bogner. 2003. *Motivating Primary-Grade Students.* New York: Guilford.

Rasinski, Timothy, David Paige, Cameron Rains, Fran Stewart, Brenda Julovich, Deb Prenkert, William H. Rupley, and William Dee Nichols. 2017. "Effects of Intensive Fluency Instruction on the Reading Proficiency of Third-Grade Struggling Readers." *Reading & Writing Quarterly* 33 (6): 519–532. doi.org/10.1080/10573569.2016.1250144.

Rupley, William H., John W. Logan, and William D. Nichols. 1999. "Vocabulary Instruction in a Balanced Reading Program." *The Reading Teacher* 52 (4), 336–346. Newark, DE: International Reading Association.

Ryder, Randall J., and Michael F. Graves. 2003. *Reading and Learning in Content Areas.* 3rd edition. Hoboken, NJ: John Wiley & Sons.

Samuels, S. Jay. 1979. "The Method of Repeated Readings." *The Reading Teacher* 32 (4): 403–408.

Santa, Carol M., Lynn T. Havens, and Bonnie J. Valdes. 1995. *Project CRISS (Creating Independence Through Student-Owned Strategies.* 3rd edition. Dubuque, IA: Kendall /Hunt.

Scarborough, Hollis S. 2001. "Connecting Early Language and Literacy to Later Reading (Dis)abilities: Evidence, Theory, and Practice." In *Handbook of Early Literacy Research,* edited by Susan B. Neuman and David K. Dickinson, 97–110. New York: Guilford.

Schwartz, Robert M., and Taffy E. Raphael. 1985. "Concept of Definition: A Key to Improving Students' Vocabulary." *The Reading Teacher* 39 (2): 198–205.

Sedita, Joan. 2019. "The Strands That Are Woven into Skilled Writing." Keys to Literacy. keystoliteracy.com/wp-content/uploads/2020/02/The-Strands-That-Are-Woven-Into -Skilled-WritingV2.pdf.

Shanahan, Timothy. 2018. "Synthetic Phonics or Systematic Phonics? What Does Research Really Say?" Reading Rockets: Shanahan on Literacy (blog), August 8, 2018. readingrockets.org/blogs/shanahan-literacy/synthetic-phonics-or-systematic-phonics -what-does-research-really-say.

Shanahan, Timothy, Kim Callison, Christine Carriere, Nell K. Duke, P. David Pearson, Christopher Schatschneider, and Joseph Torgesen. 2010. *Improving Reading Comprehension in Kindergarten through 3rd Grade: A Practice Guide* (NCEE 2010- 4038). Washington, DC: National Center for Education Evaluation and Regional Assistance, Institute of Education Sciences, U.S. Department of Education.

Shefelbine, J., and J. Calhoun. 1991. "Variability in Approaches to Identifying Polysyllabic Words: A Descriptive Study of Sixth Graders with Highly, Moderately, and Poorly Developed Syllabification Strategies." *Learner Factors/Teacher Factors: Issues in Literacy Research and Instruction,* edited by J. Zutell and S. McCormick, 169–177. Chicago: National Reading Conference.

Sinatra, Richard, Vicky Zygouris-Coe, and Sheryl B. Dasinger. 2012. "Preventing a Vocabulary Lag: What Lessons Are Learned from Research." *Reading and Writing Quarterly* 28 (4), 333–357. doi.org/10.1080/10573569.2012.702040.

Snow, Catherine E. 2018. "Simple and Not-So-Simple Views of Reading." *Remedial and Special Education* 39 (5) 313–316. doi.org/10.1177/0741932518770288.

Snow, Catherine E., and Connie Juel. 2005. "Teaching Children to Read: What Do We Know about How to Do It?" In *The Science of Reading: A Handbook*, edited by Margaret J. Snowling and Charles Hulme, 501–520. Oxford: Blackwell. doi.org/10.1002/9780470757642.ch26.

Stahl, Katherine A. Dougherty. 2014. "What Counts as Evidence?" *The Reading Teacher* 68: 103–106.

Sticht, Thomas G., and James H. James. 1984. "Listening and Reading." In *Handbook of Reading Research*, edited by P. David Pearson, with Rebecca Barr, Michael L. Kamil, and Peter Mosenthal, 293–318. New York: Routledge.

Tomlinson, Carol A. 2014. *The Differentiated Classroom: Responding to the Needs of All Learners*. 2nd edition. Alexandria, VA: ASCD.

Tompkins, Gail. 2018. *Teaching Writing: Balancing Process and Product*. 7th edition. Saddle River, NJ: Pearson.

Wanzek, Jeanne, Elizabeth A. Stevens, Kelly J. Williams, Nancy Scammacca, Sharon Vaugh, and Katherine Sargent. 2018. "Current Evidence on the Effects of Intensive Early Reading Interventions." *Journal of Learning Disabilities* 51 (6): 612–624. doi.org/10.1177/0022219418775110.

Wattenberg, Ruth. 2016. "Inside the Common Core Reading Tests: Why the Best Prep Is a Knowledge-Rich Curriculum." *Knowledge Matters*, Issue Brief #7, September 2016. knowledgematterscampaign.org/wp-content/uploads/2016/09/Wattenberg.pdf.

Wexler, Natalie. 2019. *The Knowledge Gap: The Hidden Cause of America's Broken Education System—and How to Fix It*. New York: Penguin/Random House.

Willingham, Daniel T. 2006. "How Knowledge Helps: It Speeds and Strengthens Reading Comprehension, Learning—and Thinking." *American Educator,* Spring 2006. American Federation of Teachers. aft.org/periodical/american-educator/spring-2006/how-knowledge-helps.

Wylie, Richard E., and Donald D. Durrell. 1970. "Teaching Vowels Through Phonograms." *Elementary English* 47 (6): 787–791.

Digital Resources

Accessing the Digital Resources

The digital resources can be downloaded by following these steps:

1. Go to **www.tcmpub.com/digital**

2. Use the 13-digit ISBN number to redeem the digital resources.

3. Respond to the question using the book.

4. Follow the prompts on the Content Cloud website to sign in or create a new account.

5. The content redeemed will now be on your My Content screen. Click on the product to look through the digital resources. All file resources are available for download. Select files can be previewed, opened, and shared. Any web-based content, such as videos, links, or interactive text, can be viewed and used in the browser but is not available for download.

For questions and assistance, please contact Teacher Created Materials.

> **email:** customerservice@tcmpub.com
>
> **phone:** 800-858-7339

Contents of the Digital Resources

The digital resources include the student activity pages in this book.